It's another Quality Book from CGP

This book is for anyone doing GCSE Maths at Foundation Level, with a predicted grade of D or below.
(If you're not sure what your predicted grade is, your teacher will be able to tell you.)

It's packed with useful practice questions to help you get to grips with the essential maths you'll need for the exams.

And of course, there are some daft bits to make the whole thing vaguely entertaining for you.

What CGP is all about

Our sole aim here at CGP is to produce the highest quality books — carefully written, immaculately presented and dangerously close to being funny.

Then we work our socks off to get them out to you — at the cheapest possible prices.

Contents

Section One — Numbers

Ordering Numbers 1
Addition and Subtraction 3
Adding and Subtracting Decimals 5
Multiplying by 10, 100, etc. 7
Dividing by 10, 100, etc. 8
Multiplying Without a Calculator 9
Dividing Without a Calculator 10
Special Number Sequences 11
Multiples, Factors and Primes 12
Fractions, Decimals and Percentages 15
Fractions 16
Ratios 19
Percentages 21

Section Two — Shapes and Area

Symmetry 23
Symmetry and Tessellations 24
2D Shapes 26
3D Shapes 28
Regular Polygons 29
Perimeters 30
Areas 32
Circles 35
Volume 36
Congruence and Similarity 38

Section Three — Measurements

Metric and Imperial Units 39
Conversion Factors 41
Rounding Off 42
Clock Time Questions 44
Compass Directions and Bearings 45
Maps and Map Scales 47
Maps and Directions 49
Speed 50

Section Four — Angles and Geometry

Lines and Angles 51
Measuring Angles with Protractors 52
Five Angle Rules 53
Parallel and Perpendicular Lines 56
The Four Transformations — Translation 58
The Four Transformations — Enlargement 59
The Four Transformations — Rotation 60
The Four Transformations — Reflection 61
Constructing Triangles 62

Section Five — Handling Data

Probability 64
Equal and Unequal Probabilities 65
Listing Outcomes 66
Types of Data 67
Samples and Groups 68
Questionnaires 69
Mode, Median, Mean and Range 71
Frequency Tables 74
Finding The Mean From Frequency Tables 75
Line Graphs and Pictograms 76
Two-Way Tables 78
Scatter Graphs 79
Bar Charts 81
Pie Charts 83

Section Six — Graphs

X and Y Coordinates 85
Midpoint of a Line Segment 87
Straight-Line Graphs 88
Travel Graphs 92
Conversion Graphs 94
Reading Off Graphs 95

Section Seven — Algebra

Negative Numbers 96
Powers and Letters 97
Square Roots 98
Cube Roots 99
Algebra — Simplifying 100
Algebra — Brackets 102
Number Patterns and Sequences 103
Formulas 105
Making Formulas from Words 106
Solving Equations 107

Throughout the book, the more challenging questions are marked like this: Q1

Published by CGP

Illustrated by Ruso Bradley, Lex Ward and Ashley Tyson

From original material by Richard Parsons.

Contributors:
Gill Allen, Margaret Carr, Barbara Coleman, JE Dodds, Mark Haslam, John Lyons,
C McLoughlin, Gordon Rutter, John Waller, Janet West, Dave Williams, Philip Wood.

Updated by:
Helena Hayes, Jonathan Wray, Dawn Wright.

With thanks to Katherine Craig and Ann Francis for the proofreading.

ISBN: 978 1 84762 658 5

Groovy website: www.cgpbooks.co.uk
Printed by Elanders Ltd, Newcastle upon Tyne.
Jolly bits of clipart from CorelDRAW®

Psst... photocopying this Workbook isn't allowed, even if you've got a CLA licence. Luckily, it's dead cheap, easy and quick to order more copies from CGP — just call us on 0870 750 1242. Phew!

Text, design, layout and original illustrations © Richard Parsons 2011
All rights reserved.

SECTION ONE — NUMBERS

Ordering Numbers

You need to be able to deal with big numbers. That means reading them, writing them down, and putting them in order. Let's get rocking...

Q1 Fill in the blanks below to show how the number **1 235 129** is split into its different parts:

	1 000 000	one million
	200 000	**two** hundred thousand
3,000	30 000	**three** thousand ✗ 30 thousand
	5 000	five thousand ✓
	1 00	**one** hundred ✓
	2 0	twenty ✓
	9	**nine** units ✓

Q2 Lewis is writing a cheque for **£278**.
Write this amount **in words** as it should be written on the cheque.

...........**two hundred and seventy eight**........... pounds.

Q3 Write down the following as a number:

> nine hundred and thirty one thousand, four hundred and one

................**931,401**................ ✓

Q4 Write down the **name of the column** that has the number **4** in it for each of the numbers below.

For example: 408   *hundreds*

a) 347 ....**tens**.... ✓   b) 41 ....**tens**.... ✓   c) 5478 ....**hundred**.... ✓

d) 6754 ....**units**.... ✓   e) 4897 ....**thousand**.... ✓   f) 64,098 ....**thousand**.... ✓

g) 7⑤45,320 ....**thousand**.... ✗   h) 2,402,876 ....**hundred**.... ✓   i) 6 503 428 ....**hundred**.... ✓
                                                    thousand

Ordering Numbers

Q5 Put these numbers in order from smallest to biggest.

a) 117   5   374   13   89   18

smallest: 5   13   18   89   117   374 ← Biggest ✓

b) 1272   231   376   233   46   73   1101

46   73   231   233   376   1101   1272 ✓

Q6 Fill in the blanks below to show how the number **16.321** is split into its different parts:

10.000   one ten ✓
6.000   six units ✓
0.300   three tenths ✓
0.020   two hundredths ✓
0.001   one thousandth ✓

Q7 Write down the name of the column or decimal place that has the number **2** in it for each of the numbers below.

For example: 2.081   units

a) 1.62   hundredths ~~tenths~~ ✓
b) 53.24   tenths ~~units~~ ✓
c) 4.542   thousandth ✓
d) 21.6   tens ✓
e) 2.4   units ✓
f) 0.523   hundredths ✓

Q8 Put these numbers in order of size — from smallest to biggest.

a) 3.4   0.034   0.0034   0.34

0.0034   0.034   0.34   3.4 ✓

Always look at the whole number part first, then the first digit after the decimal point, then the next, etc.

b) 6.7   6.1   0.06   0.64   0.0061

0.0061   0.06   0.64   6.1   6.7 ✓

c) 1.13   0.05   0.67   1.91   0.002

0.002   0.05   0.67   1.13   1.91 ✓

d) 1.201   1.206   12   0.021   2.20

0.021   2.20   1.201   1.206   12 ✗

SECTION ONE — NUMBERS

Addition and Subtraction

 **NO CALCULATORS HERE!** ALWAYS put the numbers in COLUMNS when you're adding... and check the UNITS, TENS and HUNDREDS line up.

Q1 **Add** these numbers together:

a) 63
   +32
   95 ✓

b) 75
   +48
   123 ✓

c) 528
   +196
   724 ✓

Q2 **Add** these numbers together. Set them out in columns first.

a) 5 + 9
   = **14** ✓

b) 26 + 15
   = **41** ✓
   (26 + 15 = 41)

c) 34 + 72
   = **106** ✓
   (34 + 72 = 106)

d) 238 + 56
   = **294** ✓
   (238 + 56 = 294)

e) 528 + 173
   = **701** ✓
   (528 + 173 = 701)

f) 215 + 2514
   = **2729** ✓
   (2514 + 215 = 2729)

Q3 **Add** together the numbers below:

a) 267
   864
   +429
   1560 ✓

b) 837
   269
   +734
   1840 ✓

c) 271
   658
   +362
   1291 ✓

Q4 Alan sold tickets for the local dance show. He wrote down his ticket sales for all three nights in this table:

How many tickets did Alan sell **in total**?

	Sales
Thursday	104
Friday	139
Saturday	122

104
139
+122
365

365 ✓

Q5 Sally bought a new car for **£11 995**. She also had to spend **£125** on road tax and **£327** on insurance. Work out the **total amount** of money she spent on the car.

11995
327
125
12447 = **12447** ✓

Addition and Subtraction

Answer the questions on this page **without** using a calculator.

Q6 **Subtract** the following:

a) 36
   −13
   23 ✓

b) 45
   −23
   22

c) 89
   −24
   65

d) ¹2̷5
   − 8
   17

e) ⁷8̷0
   −42
   38

f) ⁶7̷2
   −19
   53

Q7 **Subtract** these numbers. Set them out in columns first.

a) 687 − 235
   687
   235
   = 452

b) 754 − 538
   754
   538
   = 216

c) 843 − 516
   843
   516
   = 327

d) 634 − 98
   634
   98
   = 536

e) 908 − 325
   908
   325
   = 583

f) 650 − 317
   650
   317
   = 333

g) 830 − 293
   830
   293
   = 537

h) 700 − 248
   700
   248
   = 452

Q8 Marvin runs a race in **350 seconds**. It takes Barry **58 seconds less** than Marvin to run the race. How long does Barry take to run the race?

350
 58
292

............292...... s

Q9 Hayley has **£4127** in her bank account. She takes out **£530** for a holiday and **£328** to pay for insurance. How much does she have left?

Add together the amounts she takes out, then take this away from the amount she had to start with.

530
328
3269

£ ...3269...

SECTION ONE — NUMBERS

Adding and Subtracting Decimals

Answer the questions on this page **without** using a calculator.

Q1 **Add** these numbers together.

a) 2.4 + 3.2 = 5.6

b) 3.5 + 4.6 = 8.1

c) 6.2 + 5.9 = 12.1

d) 7.34 + 6.07 = 13.41

e) 9.08 + 4.93 = 14.01

f) 15.73 + 25.08 = 40.81

g) 26.05 + 72.95 = 99.00

Q2 Write these sums out in **columns** and add them together.

a) 3.6 + 7.3
3.6
7.3
= 10.9

b) 21.4 + 13.8
21.4
13.8
= 35.2

c) 0.9 + 5.6
0.9
5.6
= 6.5

d) 9.98 + 6.03
9.98
16.03
16.01
= 16.01

e) 2.9 + 7
2.9
7.0
= 9.9

f) 4.36 + 7.1
4.36
7.10
= 11.46

g) 9.8 + 1.05
9.80
1.05
= 10.85

h) 6 + 6.75
6.75
6.00
= 12.75

i) 0.28 + 18.5
18.50
00.28
= 18.78

j) 47.23 + 6.7
47.23
106.70
= 53.93

Q3 Work out the missing **lengths**.

a)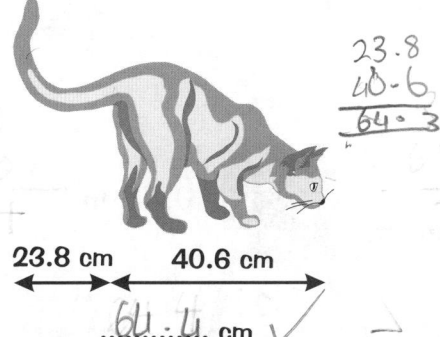

23.8 cm 40.6 cm

23.8 + 40.6 = 64.3

..64.4.. cm

b)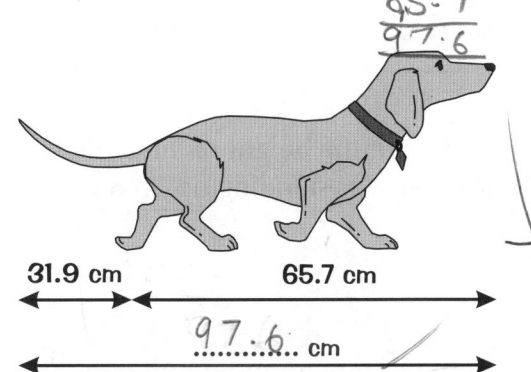

31.9
65.7
97.6

31.9 cm 65.7 cm

..97.6.. cm

Q4 Peter bought a cup of tea, a cup of coffee, a cheese burger and a bacon butty. Work out the **total cost**.

2.99
2.00
2.99
1.80
6.78

£ ..6.78..

| Tea | 80p | Cheese Burger | £2.99 |
| Coffee | 99p | Bacon Butty | £2.00 |

Write out the prices of the tea and coffee in pounds first.

SECTION ONE — NUMBERS

Adding and Subtracting Decimals

Answer the questions on this page **without** using a calculator.

Q5 **Subtract** the following.

a) 9.8
   −3.1
   6.7 ✓

b) 7.3
   −2.3
   5.0

c) 6.2
   −1.5
   4.7 ✓

d) 8.6
   −3.9
   4.7 ✓

e) 7.0
   −1.6
   5.4 ✓

f) 13.6
   −12.7
   00.9 ✓

g) 14.65
   − 4.70
   9.95 ✓

h) 8.34
   −4.65
   3.69 ✓

Q6 **Subtract** these numbers. Set them out in columns first.

a) 8.5 − 1.6
   8.5
   1.6
   = 6.9 ✓

b) 18.3 − 5.9
   18.3
   5.9
   = 12.4 ✓

c) 24.1 − 16.3
   24.1
   16.3
   = 7.8 ✓

You have to give the whole numbers a decimal point yourself, and some zeros too. E.g. 9 − 3.6 becomes 9.0 − 3.6.

d) 9 − 3.6
   9.0
   3.6
   = 5.4 ✓

e) 40 − 2.3
   40.0
   2.3
   = 37.7 ✓

f) 51 − 18.32
   51.00
   18.32
   = 32.68 ✓

Q7 Work out the **height** of the table that the television is standing on, in metres.

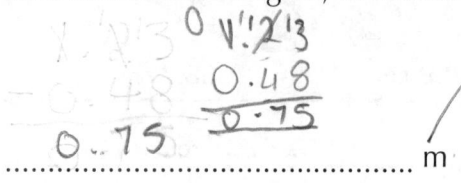

0.75 m ✓

Q8 Kate bought a jar of coffee for **£3.24** and a loaf of bread for **£1.37**. She paid for it with a **£10** note. How much change should she get?

When you're dealing with money, you've got two decimal places.

£ 5.39 ✓

SECTION ONE — NUMBERS

Multiplying by 10, 100, etc.

 Multiplying by 10, 100 or 1000 moves the decimal point 1, 2 or 3 places to the right — then you just fill in any gaps with zeros. Don't use a calculator for this page.

Q1 **Multiply** the following:

a) 8 × 10 = 80 ✓

b) 34 × 100 = 3400 ✓

c) 52 × 100 = 5200 ✓

d) 9 × 1000 = 9000 ✓

e) 436 × 1000 = 436000 ✓

f) 0.2 × 10 = 20 ✗

g) 6.9 × 10 = 69 ✓

h) 4.73 × 100 = 473 ✓

Q2 Fill in the **missing numbers**.

a) 6 × [10] = 60 ✓

b) 0.07 × [10] = 0.7 ✓

c) 6 × [100] = 600 ✓

d) 0.07 × [100] = 7 ✓

e) 6 × [1000] = 6000 ✓

f) 0.07 × [1000] = 70 ✓

Q3 For a school concert chairs are put out in rows of 10. How many chairs will be needed for **16 rows**?   160 ✓

Q4  How much do **10 chickens** cost?   £29.90 ✓

2.99 × 10
↓
29.9

Q5 A school buys calculators for **£2.45** each. How much will **100 calculators** cost?   £245 ✓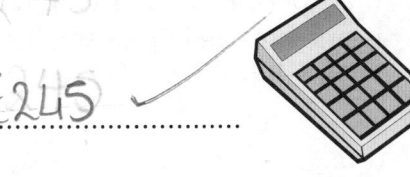

£2.45
 100

Q6 **Multiply** the following:

a) 2 × 30 = 60 ✓

b) 40 × 20 = 800 ✓

c) 250 × 400 = 100,000 ✓

d) 15 × 2000 = 30,000 ✓

Q7 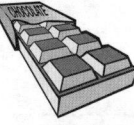 A shop bought **700** bars of chocolate for **40p** each. How much did they cost in total?   280 ✓

700 × 40
7 × 4 = 28

SECTION ONE — NUMBERS

Dividing by 10, 100, etc.

Dividing by 10, 100 or 1000 moves the decimal point 1, 2 or 3 places to the left.

Answer these questions **without** using a calculator:

Q1
a) 30 ÷ 10 = 3 ✓
b) 43 ÷ 10 = 4.3 ✓
c) 5.8 ÷ 10 = .58 ✗

d) 63.2 ÷ 10 = 6.32 ✓ [63.2]
e) 0.5 ÷ 10 = 0.05 ✓
f) 400 ÷ 100 = 4 ✓

g) 423 ÷ 100 = 4.23 ✓
h) 228.6 ÷ 100 = 2.286 ✓ [2.2816]
i) 61.5 ÷ 100 = 0.615 ✓ [0.6115]

j) 2.96 ÷ 100 = 0.0296 ✓
k) 6000 ÷ 1000 = 6 ✓
l) 6334 ÷ 1000 = 6.334 ✓

m) 753.6 ÷ 1000 = 0.7536 ✓
n) 8.15 ÷ 1000 = 00.815 ✗ [0.00815]
o) 80 ÷ 20 = 4 ✓

p) 860 ÷ 20 = 43 ✓
q) 2400 ÷ 300 = 12 ✗
r) 480 ÷ 40 = 12 ✓

s) 860 ÷ 200 = 4.3 ✓
t) 63.9 ÷ 30 = 2.13 ✓

Q2 Ten people share a Lottery win of **£62**.
How much should each person receive?

£6.20 ✓   62 ÷ 10 = 6.20

Q3 Blackpool Tower is **158 m** tall. A model of the tower is **one hundred** times smaller than this.
How tall is the model?

1.58 ✓   158 ÷ 100 = 1.58

.... m

Q4 A box of **30** chocolates contains **60 g** of fat.
How much fat is there in **1** chocolate?

2 ✓ g   30 ÷ 60

3) 60

Q5 Mark got **330 euros** for **£300** for his holiday money.
How many euros is **£1** worth?

1.1 ✓   330 ÷ 300

SECTION ONE — NUMBERS

Multiplying Without a Calculator

 There are lots of different ways you can multiply numbers. What you have to do is pick a method you like and practise using it on questions.

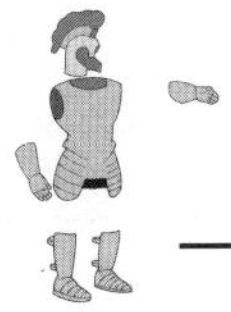

Q1 Use the **grid method** to **multiply** the following numbers:

a)
	20	1
10	200	10
1	20	1

200
10
20
1
231

21 × 11 = ...231... ✓

b)
	10	6
40	400	240
1	10	6

400
240
10
6
656

16 × 41 = ...656... ✓

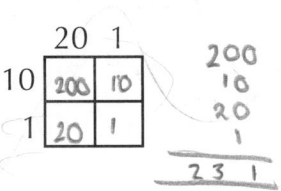

c)
	30	9
70	2100	630
2	60	18

2100
630
60
18
2808

39 × 72 = ...2808... ✓

d)
	200	10	3
7	1400	70	21

1400
70
21
1491

213 × 7 = ...1491... ✓

e)
	100	20	3
80	8000	1600	240
4	400	80	12

123 × 84 = ...10332... ✓

8000
1600
240
400
80
12
10332

Q2 **Multiply** the following without a calculator. Use any method.

a) 23 × 2

```
  23
×  2
----
  46
```
= ...46... ✓

b) 225 × 3

```
 225
   3
----
 675
```
= ...675... ✓

c) 546 × 5

```
 546
   5
----
2730
```
= ...2730... ✓

d) 126 × 14

```
  126
   14
-----
  504
 1260
-----
 1764
```
= ...1,764... ✓

e) 413 × 26

```
  413
   26
-----
 2478
 8260
-----
10738
```
= ...10738... ✓

f) 309 × 61

```
  309
   61
-----
  309
18540
-----
18849
```
= ...18849... ✓

g) 847 × 53

```
  847
   53
-----
 2541
42350
-----
44891
```
= ...44891... ✓

h) 727 × 89

```
  727
   89
-----
 6543
58160
-----
64703
```
= ...64,703... ✓

Dividing Without a Calculator

Make sure you learn the short division method and practise using it as much as you can.

Q1 Use **short division** to **divide** the following numbers:

a) 3)396 ̄132
396 ÷ 3 = ...132... ✓

b) 13)286 ̄022
286 ÷ 13 = ...22... ✓

c) 22)506 ̄023
506 ÷ 22 = ...23... ✓

d) 17)204 ̄012
204 ÷ 17 = ...12... ✓

e) 30)990 ̄033
990 ÷ 30 = ...33... ✓

f) 35)805 ̄023
805 ÷ 35 = ...23... ✓

g) 21)651 ̄031
651 ÷ 21 = ...31... ✓

h) 19)893 ̄047
893 ÷ 19 = ...47... ✓

i) 33)759 ̄023
759 ÷ 33 = ...23... ✓

Q2 Work out the following without a calculator:

a) 834 ÷ 3
3)834 ̄278
= ...278... ✓

b) 645 ÷ 5
5)645 ̄129
= ...129... ✓

c) 702 ÷ 6
6)702 ̄117
= ...117... ✓

d) 1000 ÷ 8
8)1000 ̄0125
= ...125... ✓

e) 595 ÷ 17
17)595 ̄035
= ...35... ✓

f) 768 ÷ 16
16)768 ̄042
= ...42... ✗

g) 984 ÷ 24
24)984 ̄041
= ...41... ✓

h) 672 ÷ 14
14)672 ̄048
= ...48... ✓

i) 437 ÷ 19
19)437 ̄023
= ...23... ✓

SECTION ONE — NUMBERS

Special Number Sequences

There are seven special sequences: EVEN NUMBERS, ODD NUMBERS, SQUARE NUMBERS, CUBE NUMBERS, POWERS OF 2, POWERS OF 10 and TRIANGLE NUMBERS. You really need to know them.

   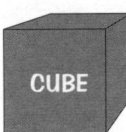 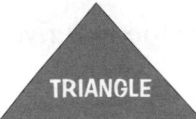

Q1 Write down what each of these **sequences** is called, and what the next term in each sequence is.

a) 2, 4, 6, 8, 10
..... Even ✓

b) 1, 3, 5, 7, 9
..... Odd ✓

c) 1, 4, 9, 16, 25
..... Square ✓

d) 1, 8, 27, 64, 125
..... Cube numbers ✓

e) 1, 3, 6, 10, 15
..... Triangle ✓

Q2

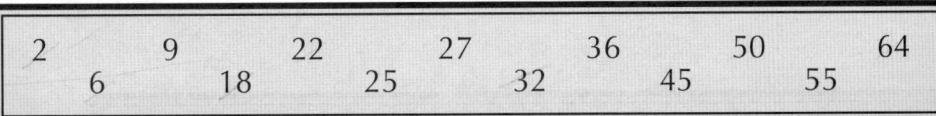

From the list above, write down:

a) All the **even** numbers 2, 6, 22, 18, 32, 50, 64, 36 ✗

b) All the **odd** numbers 9, 27, 45, 55, 25

c) All the **square** numbers 9, 25, 36, 64 ✓

d) All the **cube** numbers 27, 64

e) All the **powers of 2** 32, 64 ✓

f) All the **triangle** numbers 36, 45, 55 ✗

SECTION ONE — NUMBERS

Multiples, Factors and Primes

 The <u>multiples</u> of a number are its times table.
<u>Factors</u> are numbers that divide into a number.
<u>Prime</u> numbers don't come up in times tables (other than their own).

Q1 What are the **first five multiples** of:

a) 4? 4, 8, 12, 16, 20

b) 7? 7, 14, 21, 28, 35

c) 11? 11, 22, 33, 44, 55

d) 12? 12, 24, 36, 48, 60

e) 15? 15, 30, 45, 60, 75

Q2 Write down all the **multiples** of 3 that are **less than 20**.

3, 6, 9, 12, 15, 18

Q3

| 14 | 20 | 22 | 35 | 50 | 55 | 70 | 77 | 99 |

Which of the numbers in the box above are **multiples** of:

a) 2? 20, 14, 22

b) 5? 50, 55, 20, 70, 35

c) 7? 70, 77, 14

d) 11? 22, 55, 77, 99

Q4

| 14 | 17 | 21 | 28 | 37 | 56 | 60 | 65 | 77 | 84 |

Which of the numbers in the box above are **not multiples** of 7?

17, 37, 60, 65

Q5 Circle all the **factors** of 36 in this list of numbers.

(1) (2) (3) (4) 5 (6) 7 8 (9) 10

Q6 Circle all the **factors** of 60 in this list of numbers.

(1) (2) (3) (4) (5) (6) 7 8 9 (10) 11 12 13 14 (15)

Section One — Numbers

Multiples, Factors and Primes

Q7 List all the **factors** of the following numbers.

a) 18 1, 2, 3, 6, 9, 18

b) 22 1, 2, 11, 22

c) 35 1, 5, ~~3~~, 7, 35

d) 7 1, 7

e) 16 1, 2, 4, 8, 16

f) 49 1, 7, 49

g) 32 1, 4, 8, 32

h) 31 1, 31

i) 50 1, 2, 5, 10

j) 62 1, 2, 31, 62

k) 81 1, 3, 9, 27, 81

l) 100 1, 2, 4, 5, 10, 100

Q8 Write down the first **ten prime numbers**.

2, 3, 5, 7, 11, 13, 17, 19, 23, 29

Q9

| 31 | 2 | 25 | 15 | 18 | 64 | 100 | 5 | 55 |
| 44 | 3 | 7 | 29 | 4 | | 50 | 11 | 37 |

Write down all the **prime numbers** from the list above.

2, 3, 5, 7, 11, 29, 31, 37

Q10 Explain why **27** is **not** a **prime number**.

27 is not a prime number because it can be multiplied by 3

Q11 Is **35** a **prime number**? Give a reason for your answer.

No because it can be multiplied by 5 and 7 whereas a prime number can only be multiplied by 1 and its self.

Multiples, Factors and Primes

Q12 17 students are going on a school trip. Is there a way of splitting the students into groups of **equal numbers**? Give a reason for your answer.

....

Q13 **24** sumo wrestlers are organised into teams of **equal numbers**. Circle the possible numbers of wrestlers in **each team** from the list below.

2   3   4   5   6   7   8   9   10   11   12

To answer this question, you need to find all the factors of 24.

Q14
a) I am a **factor** of **24**.
I am an **odd** number.
I am **bigger than 1**.
What number am I?
....

b) I am a **factor** of **30**.
I am an **even** number.
I am **less than 5**.
What number am I?
....

c) I am a **prime** number.
I am an **even** number.
What number am I?
....

d) I am a **multiple** of **3**.
I am an **even** number.
I am **less than 10**.
What number am I?
....

Q15 Stephen is buying cheese straws for a dinner party. There will be **7** people at the dinner party. Cheese straws come in packs of **35** or packs of **50**. He wants to be able to share the cheese straws out **equally**.

a) Which size pack should he buy? ....

b) How many cheese straws will each person get? ....

SECTION ONE — NUMBERS

Fractions, Decimals and Percentages

Q1 Change these fractions to **decimals**:

a) $\frac{1}{2}$ .... b) $\frac{3}{4}$ .... c) $\frac{7}{10}$ .... d) $\frac{19}{20}$ ....

e) $\frac{1}{100}$ .... f) $\frac{4}{5}$ .... g) $\frac{1}{25}$ .... h) $\frac{1}{3}$ ....

Q2 Change these fractions to **percentages**:

a) $\frac{1}{4}$ .... b) $\frac{3}{10}$ .... c) $\frac{4}{5}$ .... d) $\frac{12}{25}$ ....

e) $\frac{8}{100}$ .... f) $\frac{2}{40}$ .... g) $\frac{1}{20}$ .... h) $\frac{1}{50}$ ....

Q3 Change these decimals to **percentages**:

a) 0.62 .... b) 0.74 .... c) 0.4 .... d) 0.9 ....

e) 0.07 .... f) 0.02 .... g) 0.12 .... h) 0.98 ....

Q4 Change these percentages to **decimals**:

a) 25% .... b) 49% .... c) 3% .... d) 30% ....

Q5 Change these percentages to **fractions**. Cancel down the fractions where you can.

a) 75% .... b) 60% .... c) 15% .... d) 24% ....

Q6 Change these decimals to **fractions**. Cancel down the fractions where you can.

a) 0.5 .... b) 0.8 .... c) 0.18 .... d) 0.25 ....

e) 0.46 .... f) 0.06 .... g) 0.12 .... h) 0.74 ....

FRACTIONS, DECIMALS AND PERCENTAGES
are all just different ways of saying "a bit of" something.

SECTION ONE — NUMBERS

Fractions

To make an EQUIVALENT fraction, you've got to multiply the TOP and BOTTOM by the SAME THING.

Q1 Shade in the correct number of sections to make these fractions **equivalent**.

$\frac{1}{4} =$

$\frac{1}{3} =$

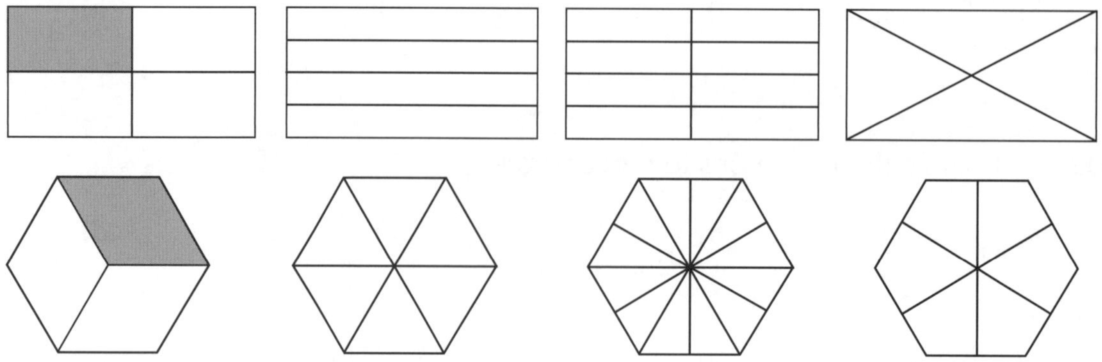

Q2 Write in the missing numbers to **cancel down** these fractions.

For example $\frac{7}{14} = \frac{1}{2}$

a) $\frac{4}{16} = \frac{1}{\square}$ b) $\frac{9}{12} = \frac{3}{\square}$ c) $\frac{2}{6} = \frac{\square}{3}$

d) $\frac{8}{12} = \frac{2}{\square}$ e) $\frac{6}{18} = \frac{1}{\square}$ f) $\frac{24}{32} = \frac{3}{\square}$

Q3 Write in the missing numbers to make all the fractions in each list **equivalent**.

a) $\frac{1}{2} = \frac{2}{\square} = \frac{\square}{6} = \frac{\square}{8} = \frac{5}{10} = \frac{25}{\square} = \frac{\square}{70} = \frac{\square}{100}$

b) $\frac{200}{300} = \frac{100}{\square} = \frac{\square}{15} = \frac{40}{\square} = \frac{120}{180} = \frac{\square}{9} = \frac{\square}{3}$

c) $\frac{7}{10} = \frac{14}{\square} = \frac{\square}{30} = \frac{210}{\square} = \frac{49}{\square} = \frac{\square}{20}$

d) $\frac{19}{20} = \frac{\square}{80} = \frac{38}{\square} = \frac{57}{\square} = \frac{\square}{100} = \frac{\square}{1000}$

Q4 Write these sets of fractions in **order of size**, from smallest to biggest:

Put them over the same number first.

a) $\frac{1}{5}, \frac{3}{10}$ .... b) $\frac{3}{7}, \frac{6}{21}$ ....

c) $\frac{11}{15}, \frac{4}{6}, \frac{4}{5}$ .... d) $\frac{1}{3}, \frac{5}{12}, \frac{4}{6}$ ....

SECTION ONE — NUMBERS

Fractions

Dealing with fractions is a lot easier if you've learned the rules:

- **MULTIPLYING:** multiply the top numbers then multiply the bottom numbers.
- **DIVIDING:** turn the second fraction upside down, then multiply them.
- **ADDING OR SUBTRACTING:**
  1) Make the bottom numbers the same.
  2) Add or subtract the top numbers only.
- **FINDING A FRACTION OF SOMETHING:**
  Multiply by the top number, then divide by the bottom number.

Answer the following questions **without** using a calculator.

Q5 **Multiply** these fractions. Give your answers in their simplest form.

a) $\frac{4}{3} \times \frac{3}{4}$ .... b) $\frac{2}{5} \times \frac{3}{5}$ ....

c) $\frac{2}{5} \times \frac{3}{4}$ .... d) $\frac{6}{7} \times \frac{7}{9}$ ....

e) $\frac{9}{11} \times \frac{6}{5}$ .... f) $\frac{2}{15} \times \frac{10}{3}$ ....

Simplest form means they're cancelled down as far as possible.

Q6 **Divide** these fractions. Give your answers in their simplest form.

a) $\frac{1}{4} \div \frac{3}{8}$ .... b) $\frac{3}{2} \div \frac{12}{5}$ ....

c) $\frac{1}{9} \div \frac{2}{3}$ .... d) $\frac{4}{5} \div \frac{9}{10}$ ....

e) $\frac{5}{12} \div \frac{5}{4}$ .... f) $\frac{4}{11} \div \frac{5}{11}$ ....

Q7 **Add** these fractions, giving your answers in their simplest form:

a) $\frac{4}{8} + \frac{3}{8}$ .... b) $\frac{1}{12} + \frac{5}{12}$ .... c) $\frac{1}{3} + \frac{2}{3}$ ....

d) $\frac{1}{6} + \frac{1}{6}$ .... e) $\frac{1}{2} + \frac{1}{4}$ .... f) $\frac{3}{10} + \frac{2}{5}$ ....

Q8 **Subtract** these fractions, giving your answers in their simplest form:

a) $\frac{11}{4} - \frac{9}{4}$ .... b) $\frac{10}{3} - \frac{8}{3}$ .... c) $\frac{7}{10} - \frac{3}{10}$ ....

d) $\frac{14}{9} - \frac{7}{9}$ .... e) $\frac{3}{2} - \frac{3}{4}$ .... f) $\frac{5}{8} - \frac{1}{4}$ ....

SECTION ONE — NUMBERS

Fractions

Q9 Work out the following amounts:

a) **Half** of 12 = ...   b) **Quarter** of 24 = ...   c) **Third** of 30 = ...

d) $\frac{1}{4}$ of 44 = ...   e) $\frac{1}{5}$ of 60 = ...   f) $\frac{2}{3}$ of 6 = ...

Q10 **Fill in the blanks** to work out the following amounts.
Do not use a calculator for this question.

e.g. $\frac{1}{3}$ of 18 = 18 ÷ 3 = <u>6</u>

a) $\frac{1}{8}$ of 32 = ... ÷ 8 = ...   b) $\frac{1}{10}$ of 50 = ... ÷ 10 = ...

c) $\frac{1}{12}$ of 144 = ... ÷ .... = ...   d) $\frac{1}{25}$ of 75 = ... ÷ .... = ...

e) $\frac{1}{30}$ of 180 = ... ÷ .... = ...   f) $\frac{1}{27}$ of 270 = ... ÷ .... = ...

Q11 **Fill in the blanks** to work out the following fractions.
Do not use a calculator for this question.

e.g. $\frac{2}{5}$ of 50   2 × 50 = 100   100 ÷ 5 = 20

a) $\frac{2}{3}$ of 60   2 × 60 = 120   120 ÷ 3 = ...

b) $\frac{4}{5}$ of 25   4 × 25 = ... ÷ 5 = ...

c) $\frac{1}{9}$ of 63   .... × 63 = ... ÷ .... = ...

d) $\frac{3}{10}$ of 100   .... × .... = ... ÷ .... = ...

e) $\frac{2}{19}$ of 19   .... × .... = ... ÷ .... = ...

f) $\frac{2}{9}$ of 18   .... × .... = ... ÷ .... = ...

g) $\frac{2}{18}$ of 90   .... × .... = ... ÷ .... = ...

Q12 Peter works in a clothes shop. He gets a staff discount and only has to pay $\frac{1}{3}$ of the price of any item. How much will a **£24** top cost him?

....

Q13 A car journey uses $\frac{2}{3}$ of a tank of petrol. How much does the journey cost, if it costs **£54** for a **full tank** of petrol?

....

SECTION ONE — NUMBERS

Ratios

Don't forget the Golden Rule...
DIVIDE FOR ONE, THEN TIMES FOR ALL.

Q1 What is the **ratio** in each of these pictures?

a)

Circles to triangles   Triangles to circles

.... : .... : ....

b)

Big stars to small stars

.... : ....

Q2 It costs **£3.60** to buy **3** loaves of bread.

a) How much does **1** loaf cost? ....

b) How much would **4** loaves cost? ....

Q3 It takes Betty **4 hours** to walk **8 miles**.
How long would it have taken her to walk **6 miles**?

Find out how long it takes her to walk 1 mile first.

....

Q4 In a café, **4** waitresses can serve **16** tables between them.
How many tables could **7** waitresses serve?

....

SECTION ONE — NUMBERS

Ratios

Q5 **Divide** the following amounts in the given ratio.
For example:

£400 in the ratio 1 : 4   1 + 4 = 5   £400 ÷ 5 = £80

 1 × £80 = £80 and 4 × £80 = £320   £80 : £320

a) 100 g in the ratio 1 : 4   ....
.... g : .... g

b) 500 m in the ratio 2 : 3   ....
.... m : .... m

c) £12 000 in the ratio 1 : 2   ....
.... £............ : £............

d) 6.3 kg in the ratio 3 : 4   ....
.... kg : .... kg

e) £8.10 in the ratio 4 : 5   ....
.... £....... : £.......

Q6 Adam and Mags win **£24 000**. They split the money in the ratio **1 : 5**. How much does Adam get?

....

In this question, Adam gets 1 part and Mags gets 5 parts.

Q7 Write each of these ratios in its **simplest form**. The first one is done for you.

a) 4 : 6   b) 15 : 21   c) 14 : 42   d) 72 : 45

2 : 3   ...... : .... : .... : ......

A great way to check your answer when splitting things into ratios is to add up the individual amounts — they should add up to the original amount.

Section One — Numbers

Percentages

1) "OF" means "×".
2) "PER CENT" means "OUT OF 100".

Example: 30% of 150 would be
$\frac{30}{100} \times 150 = 45$.

Q1 **Without** using a calculator, work out the following amounts:

a) 50% of £12: .... = £..........

b) 20% of £20: .... = £..........

c) 10% of £50: .... = £..........

d) 5% of £50: .... = £..........

e) 30% of £50: .... = £..........

f) 20% of £80: .... = £..........

g) 10% of 90 cm: .... = ... cm

h) 10% of 4.39 kg: .... = ... kg

First divide by 10 to find 10%, then multiply or divide to find the percentage you are asked for.

Q2 Now use your **calculator** to work out these amounts:

a) 8% of £16 = ... = £..........

b) 85% of 740 kg = ... = ... kg

c) 40% of 40 minutes = ... = ... minutes

d) 25% of 64 cm = ... = ... cm

e) 35% of 400 g = ... = ... g

f) 12% of 150 m = ... = ... m

Q3 A school has **750** pupils.

a) If **60%** of the pupils are boys, what **percentage** are girls? ....

b) **How many boys** are there in the school? ....

c) One day, **10%** of the pupils were absent.
How many pupils was this? ....

d) **45%** of the pupils have a school lunch, **35%** bring sandwiches and the rest go home for lunch. **How many** pupils go home for lunch?

....

SECTION ONE — NUMBERS

Percentages

Q4 Work out these **percentage** questions:

a) A t-shirt is priced at **£18**. Ted has a **20% off** voucher to use in the shop. How much will the t-shirt cost Ted if he uses his voucher?

....

b) Susan puts **£200** in the bank. She makes **2%** interest on her money. How much interest does she make?

....

Q5 Molly buys a painting for **£90**. She then sells the painting, making a profit of **5%**. How much does she sell the painting for?

Find 5% of the original price, then add it on to the original price.

....

Q6 At a football match, there were **8000** people in the crowd. At the next match, there was a **9% decrease** in the number of people in the crowd. How many people were in the crowd at the second match?

Find the decrease, then take it from the original amount.

....

Q7

SPECIAL OFFER: All holidays 30% off original price

Justin booked a holiday on the special offer above.
The original price of the holiday was **£650**.
How much did Justin pay for the holiday?

....

Q8 Admission to a theme park is **£18** for adults. A child's ticket is **60%** of the adult price.

a) How much will it cost for **1 adult** and **4 children** to get in to the theme park?

....

b) How much will **2 adults** and **3 children** spend on entrance tickets?

....

SECTION ONE — NUMBERS

SECTION TWO — SHAPES AND AREA

Symmetry

 A shape is symmetrical if you can draw a mirror line so that the sides fold exactly together. The mirror line is called the line of symmetry.

Q1 These shapes have more than one line of symmetry.
Draw the **lines of symmetry** using dotted lines.

a) 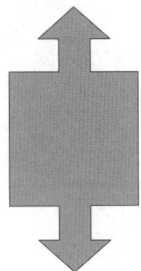   b)    c)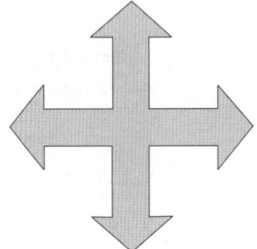

Q2 Some of the letters below have **lines of symmetry**.
Draw all the lines of symmetry using dotted lines.

A B C D E F G H I J K L M

Q3 Write down the order of **rotational symmetry** of each of the following shapes:

The order of rotational symmetry is the number of different ways a shape can look the same when you rotate it (turn it).

a)
square
....

b)
rectangle
....

c)
equilateral triangle
....

d)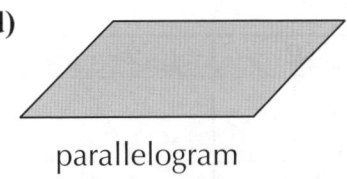
parallelogram
....

SECTION TWO — SHAPES AND AREA

Symmetry and Tessellations

Use tracing paper to help with questions on symmetry and tessellations.

Q1 **Reflect** these shapes in the given mirror line.

a) [grid with shape and horizontal mirror line]

b)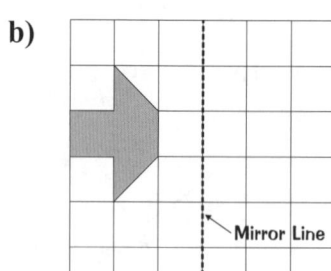

c)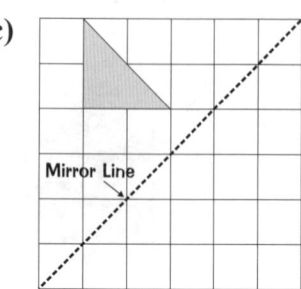

Q2 Write down the **order of rotational symmetry** of the shapes below.

a) [grid with two triangles and a line]

b)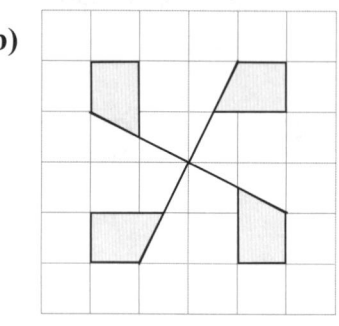

c)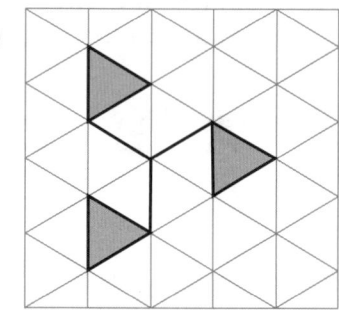

....

Q3 Draw the **line of symmetry** on these shapes:

a)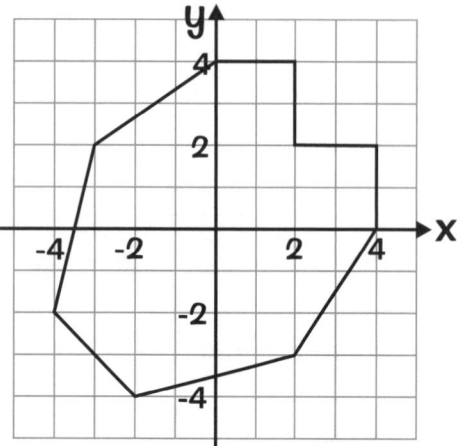

b)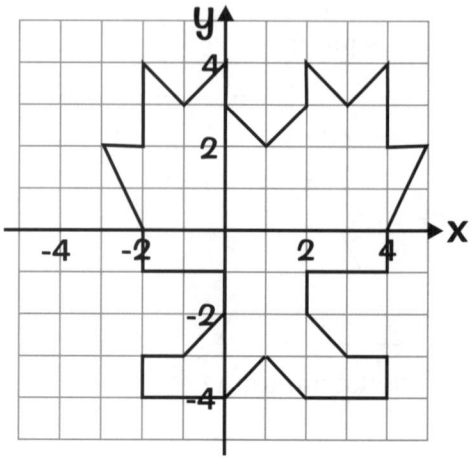

SECTION TWO — SHAPES AND AREA

Symmetry and Tessellations

Q4 A **tessellation** is a tiling pattern with **no gaps**. Continue the tessellations shown on the grid below by drawing **5 more** of each tile.

Use tracing paper to help with tessellation questions.

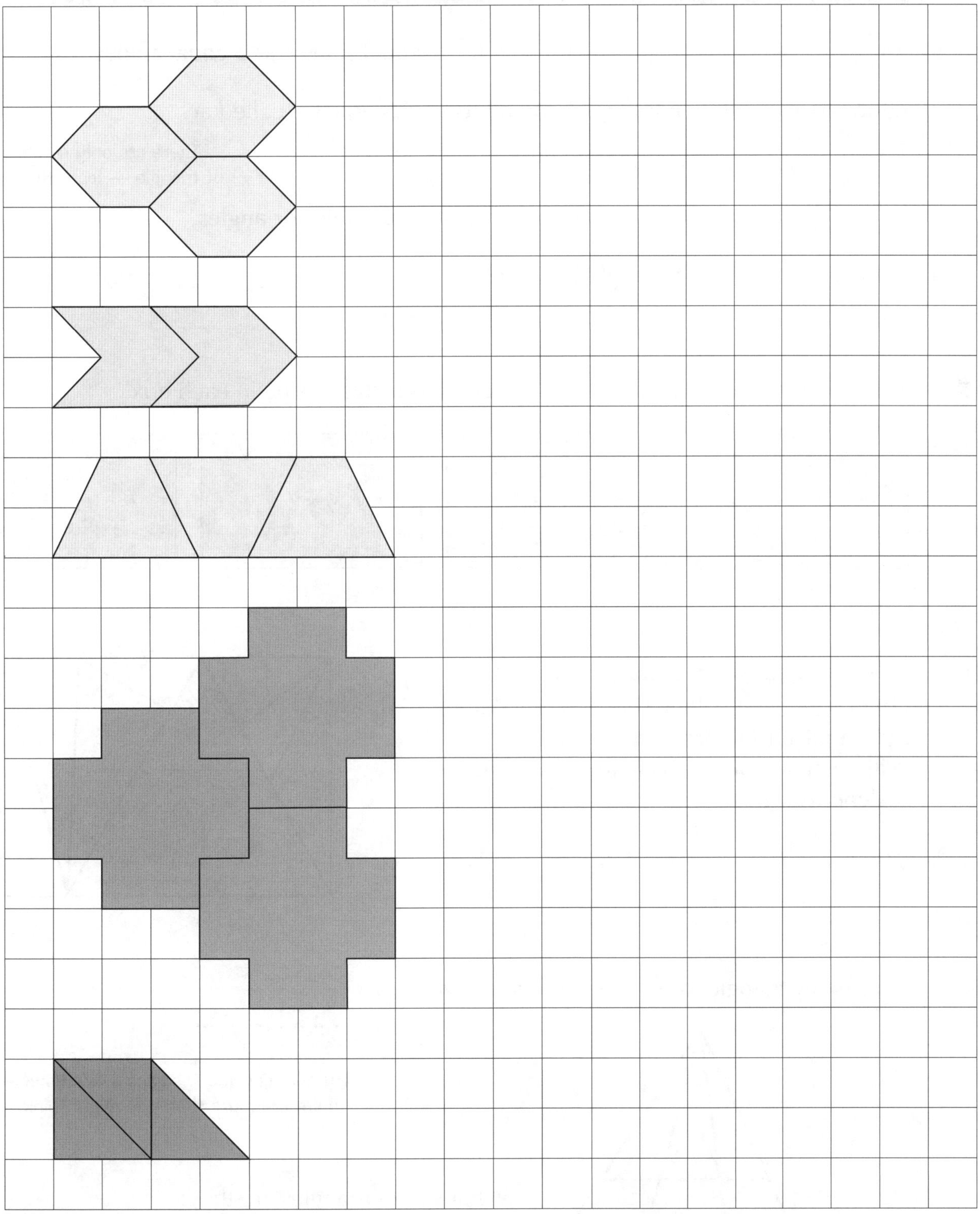

SECTION TWO — SHAPES AND AREA

2D Shapes

Q1 Complete the sentences by choosing the correct word from the box.

| equilateral | right-angled | isosceles | scalene |

a) An .... triangle has **2 equal sides** and **2 equal angles**.

b) A triangle with **all its sides equal** and **all its angles equal** is called an .... triangle.

There are only 4 types of triangle — learn them all.

c) A .... triangle has **no equal sides or angles**.

d) A triangle with one **right-angle** is called a .... triangle.

Q2 By joining dots, draw four different **isosceles triangles** — one in each box.

Q3 Find an **equilateral triangle** and shade it in.
Using a different colour, shade in two different **right-angled triangles**.
With another colour, shade in two different **scalene triangles**.

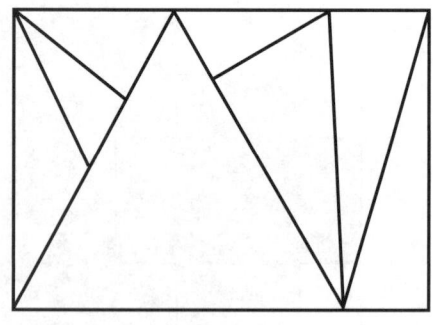

Q4 How many triangles are there in the diagram below?

....

Try counting the triangles a few times — there are more than you might think...

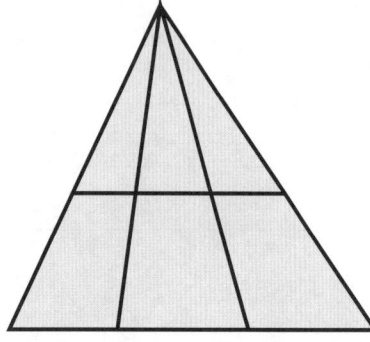

What sort of triangles are they?

....

SECTION TWO — SHAPES AND AREA

2D Shapes

Q5 Fill in the blanks in the table.

 There are a few shapes that you'll need to know about in the exam. Make sure you learn the different facts about them.

NAME	DRAWING	DESCRIPTION
Square		4 lines of symmetry. Rotational symmetry order 4.
Rectangle		2 lines of symmetry. Rotational symmetry order 2.
....		...... lines of symmetry. Rotational symmetry order ...... 2 pairs of parallel sides.
Trapezium		Only .... sides are parallel.
Rhombus		A parallelogram but with all sides ....
Kite		1 line of symmetry. No rotational symmetry.

SECTION TWO — SHAPES AND AREA

3D Shapes

Q1 Write the name of each **3D shape** on the line below it.
Choose words from the box.

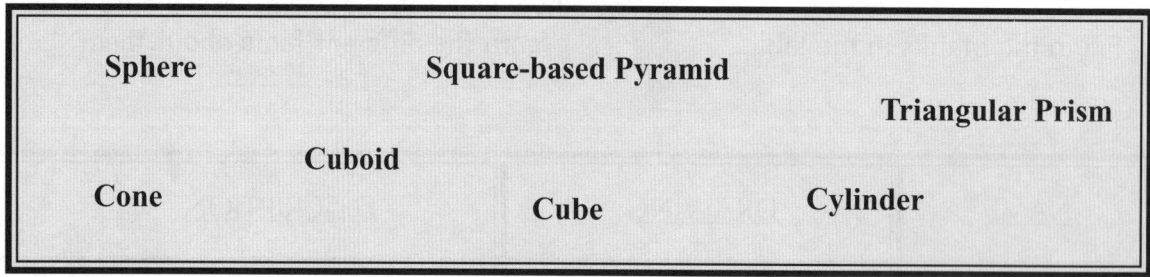

a)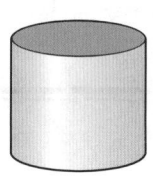

....

b)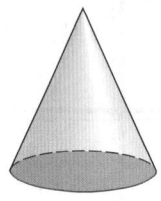

....

c)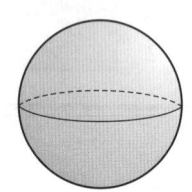

....

d)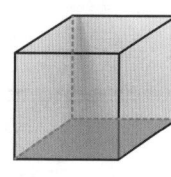

....

e)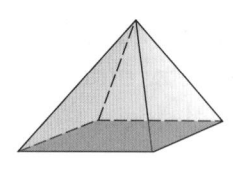

....

f)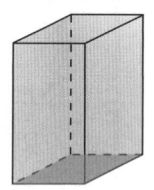

....

g)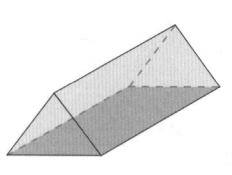

....

Q2 For each shape, write down whether it is a **prism**, or **not a prism**.

a)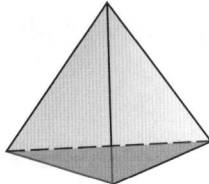

....

b)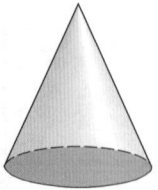

....

c)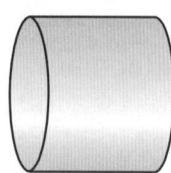

....

d)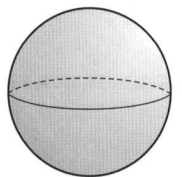

....

e)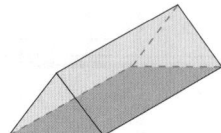

....

f)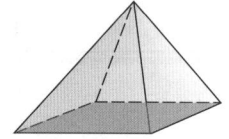

....

SECTION TWO — SHAPES AND AREA

Regular Polygons

Regular polygons are just shapes that follow certain rules.

Q1 Fill in the missing words to say what a **regular polygon** is.

> A regular polygon is a shape where all
> the .... and .... are ....

Q2 a) Sketch a **regular hexagon** in the space below.
b) Draw in all of its **lines of symmetry**.
c) State the **order of rotational symmetry**.

Rotational symmetry is just the number of positions in which the shape looks the same.

Order of rotational symmetry is ....

Q3 Complete the following table:

Name	Sides	Lines of Symmetry	Order of Rotational Symmetry
Equilateral Triangle			
Square		4	
Regular Pentagon			
Regular Hexagon	6		
Regular Heptagon	7		
Regular Octagon			8

SECTION TWO — SHAPES AND AREA

Perimeters

 Perimeter is the distance around the outside of a shape. To find the perimeter, you have to add up all the sides. You may have to sketch the shape first.

Q1 Work out the **perimeters** of the following shapes:

Fill in any missing side lengths first.

a)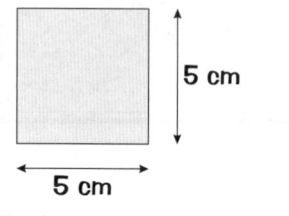

Square Perimeter = ... cm

b)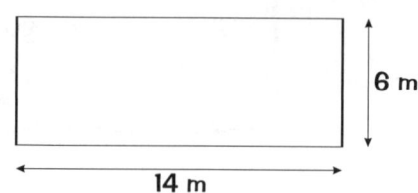

Rectangle Perimeter = ... m

c)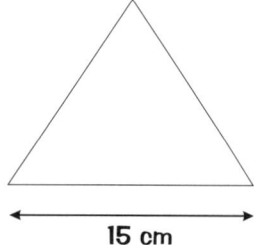

Equilateral Triangle Perimeter = ... cm

d)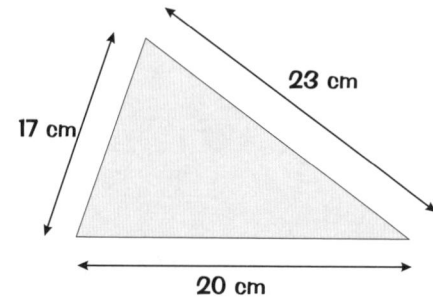

Triangle Perimeter = ... cm

e)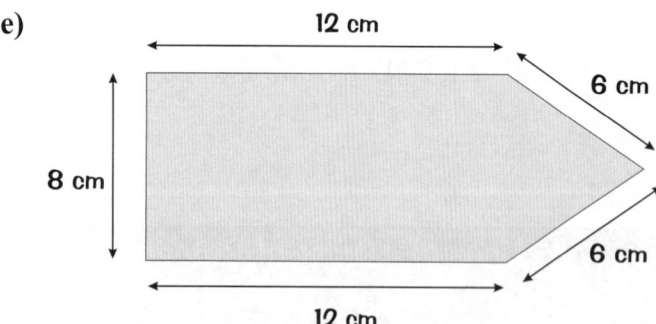

Perimeter = ... cm

f)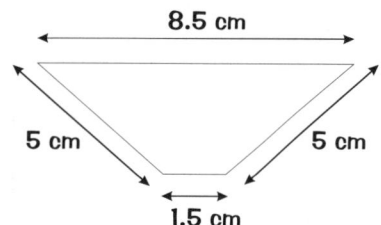

Perimeter = ... cm

Q2 A **square** garden has sides of length **10 m**.
What is the perimeter of the garden? .... m

SECTION TWO — SHAPES AND AREA

Perimeters

Q3 Find the perimeter of these shapes (you may need to work out some of the lengths):

Give units with your answers.

a)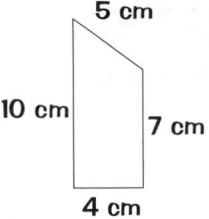

Perimeter ....

b)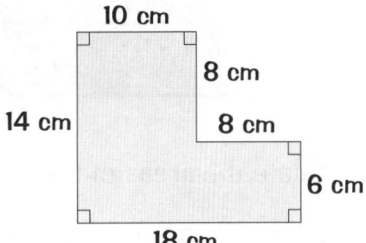

Perimeter ....

c)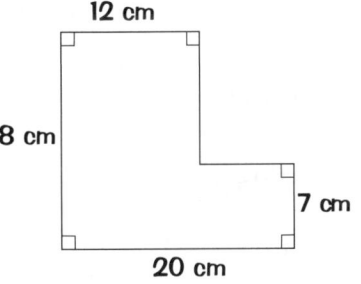

Perimeter ....

d)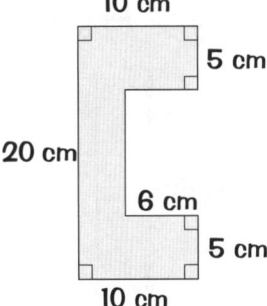

Perimeter ....

Q4 The diagram shows the floor plan of Isaac's living room.

What is the **perimeter** of his living room?

....

Work out any missing lengths first.

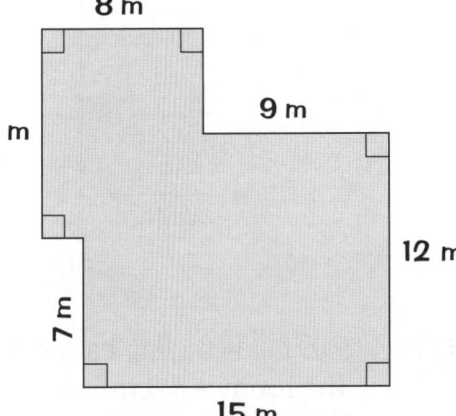

SECTION TWO — SHAPES AND AREA

Areas

You need to know the formula for finding the areas of rectangles.

| Area of a Rectangle = Length × Width |

Q1 Calculate the **areas** of the following **rectangles**:

a) Length = 10 cm, Width = 4 cm, Area = ... × ..... = ... cm².

b) Length = 55 cm, Width = 19 cm, Area = ... cm².

c) Length = 155 m, Width = 28 m, Area = ... m².

d) Length = 3.7 km, Width = 10 km, Area = ... km².

Q2 Measure the **lengths** and **widths** of each of these rectangles, then calculate the **area**.

a)
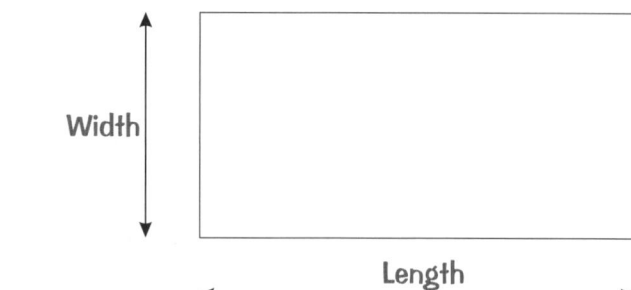

Width = ... cm

Length = ... cm

Area =

.... cm²

b)
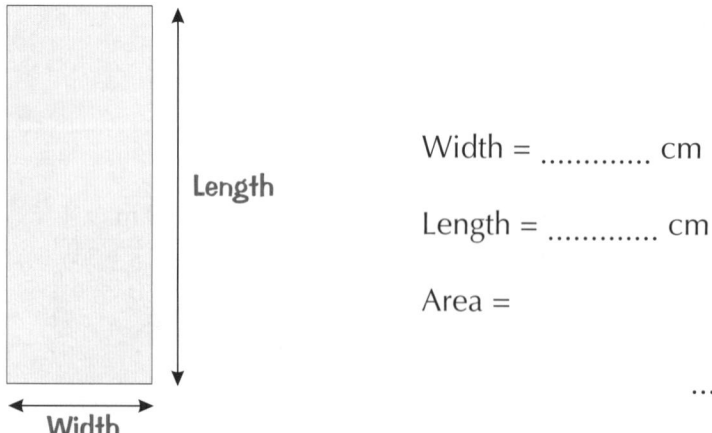

Width = ... cm

Length = ... cm

Area =

.... cm²

Q3 Sabrina is buying carpet for a **rectangular** room in her house.
The room is **4.8 m** long and **3.9 m** wide.
What **area** of carpet does she need in m²?

....

SECTION TWO — SHAPES AND AREA

Areas

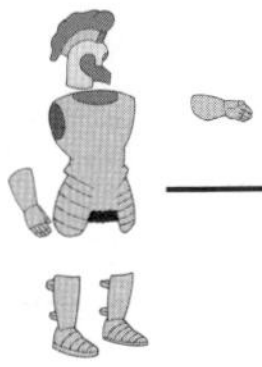

You also need to know how to work out the area of a triangle.

Area of a Triangle = ½ × Base × Vertical Height

Q4 Calculate the **areas** of the following **triangles**:

a) Base = 12 cm, Height = 9 cm, Area = ½ × .... × .... = ... cm².

b) Base = 5 cm, Height = 3 cm, Area = ... cm².

c) Base = 25 m, Height = 7 m, Area = ... m².

d) Base = 1.6 m, Height = 6.4 m, Area = ... m².

e) Base = 700 cm, Height = 350 cm, Area = ... cm².

Q5 Measure the **base** and **height** of each of these triangles, then calculate the **area**.

a)

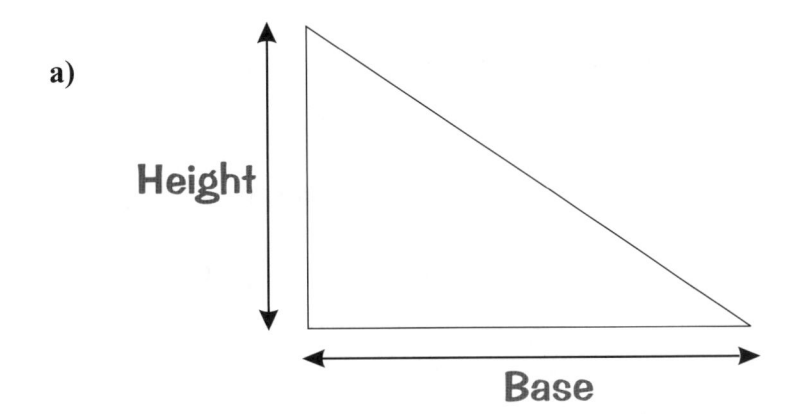

Height = ... cm

Base = ... cm

Area =

.... cm²

b)

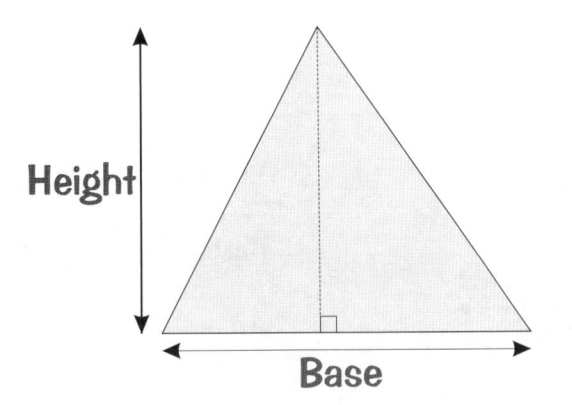

Height = ... cm

Base = ... cm

Area =

.... cm²

SECTION TWO — SHAPES AND AREA

Areas

You'll need to know the formula for the area of a parallelogram for your exam. Make sure you learn it.

Area of a Parallelogram = Base × Vertical Height

Q6 Calculate the **areas** of the following parallelograms:

a) Base = 2 cm, Vertical height = 7 cm, Area = ... × .... = ... cm².

b) Base = 3 cm, Vertical height = 4 cm, Area = ... cm².

c) Base = 15 m, Vertical height = 3 m, Area = ... m².

d) Base = 2.1 m, Vertical height = 1.5 m, Area = ... m².

e) Base = 71 cm, Vertical height = 30 cm, Area = ... cm².

Q7 Measure the **base** and **vertical height** of each of these parallelograms, then calculate the **area**.

a)

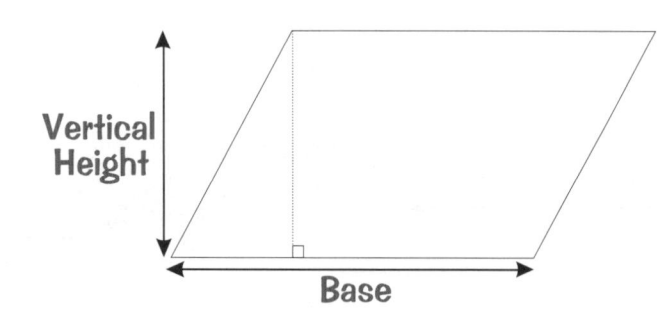

Vertical Height = ... cm

Base = ... cm

Area =

.... cm²

b)

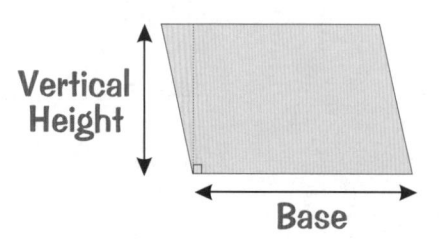

Vertical Height = ... cm

Base = ... cm

Area =

.... cm²

Circles

That π bit just stands for the number 3.14159... Sometimes you'll be told to round it off to 3.14 or 3.142. If not, use the π button on your calculator.

Q1 In the space below, draw a circle with **radius 3 cm**.
On your circle label the **circumference**, **radius** and **diameter**.

Q2 Calculate the **circumference** of these circles.
Take π to be **3.14**.

a) 2 cm

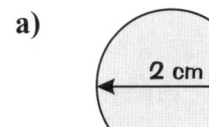

Circumference = π × diameter = ... cm

b) Circumference = π × diameter = ... cm

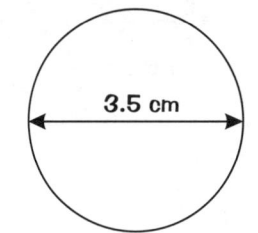

3.5 cm

c) 2.5 cm

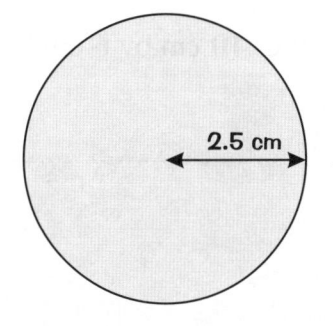

Work out the diameter first.

Diameter = radius × 2 = ... cm

Circumference = ... cm

d) A circle of radius 3.5 cm.

= .... cm

SECTION TWO — SHAPES AND AREA

Volume

Finding volumes of cubes and cuboids is just like finding areas of squares and rectangles — except you've got an extra side to multiply by.

Q1 A match box measures 7 cm by 4 cm by 5 cm. What is its **volume**?

.... cm³

Q2 What is the volume of a **cube** which has sides of length:

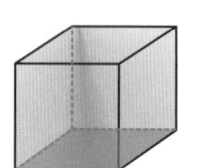

A cube has all its sides the same length.

a) 5 cm? .... cm³

b) 9 cm? .... cm³

c) 15 cm? .... cm³

Q3 Is the jelly mould on the right big enough to hold **1600 cm³** of jelly?

....

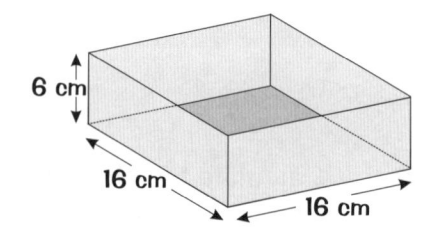

Q4 A box measures **9 cm** by **5 cm** by **8 cm**.

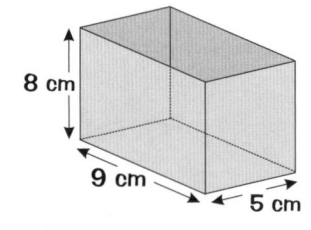

a) What is its volume? .... cm³

b) What is the volume of a box twice as long, twice as wide and twice as tall?

.... cm³

Q5 Box A measures **12 cm** by **5 cm** by **8 cm**. Box B measures **10 cm** by **6 cm** by **9 cm**. Which box has the bigger volume?

....

Q6 A rectangular swimming pool is **12 m** wide and **18 m** long. What volume of water is needed to fill the pool to a height of **2 m**?

.... m³

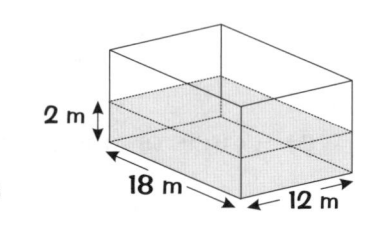

SECTION TWO — SHAPES AND AREA

Volume

Prisms are solid shapes which are the same shape all the way through. If you know the cross-sectional area and length of a prism, then you can find its volume with the formula below.

Volume of prism = Cross-sectional Area × Length

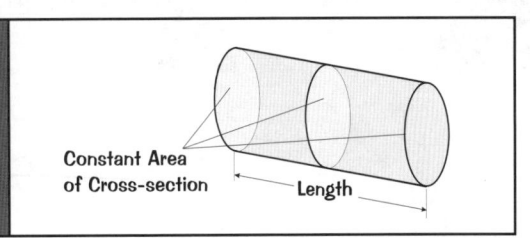

Constant Area of Cross-section — Length

Q7 A cylinder has cross-sectional area **5 cm²** and length **6 cm**. What is the cylinder's volume in cm³?

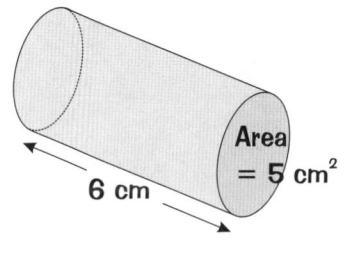

....

Q8 What are the **volumes** of the prisms with these cross-sectional areas and lengths?

a) Cross-sectional area = 2 cm², length = 4 cm. .... cm³

b) Cross-sectional area = 1.5 m², length = 8 m. .... m³

c) Cross-sectional area = 1.1 cm², length = 10 cm. .... cm³

d) Cross-sectional area = 2 cm², length = 1.2 cm. .... cm³

e) Cross-sectional area = 5 cm², length = 4.8 cm. .... cm³

Q9 A right-angled triangular prism has the side lengths shown. Find the volume of the prism in cm³.

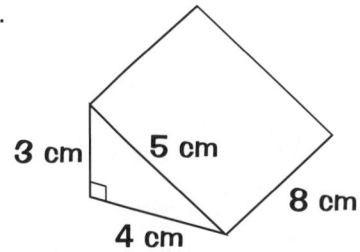

You'll need to find the cross-sectional area first.

3 cm   5 cm   8 cm   4 cm

....

....

SECTION TWO — SHAPES AND AREA

Congruence and Similarity

For the following sets of shapes, underline the one which is **not congruent** to the others.

Q1 a)   b) 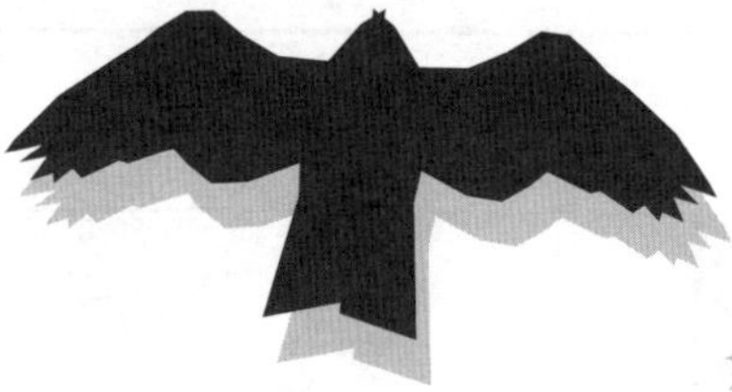   c)    d)

Q2 a)    b)    c)    d)

Q3 Trapezium B, shown below, is **similar** to trapezium A.
What does this tell you about the angles in trapezium B?

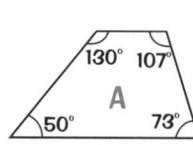

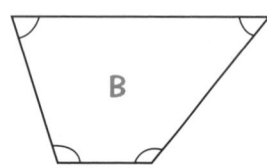

....

Q4 Are the two triangles **similar**? Give a reason for your answer.

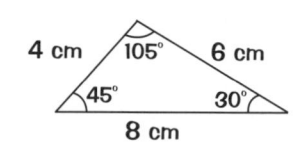

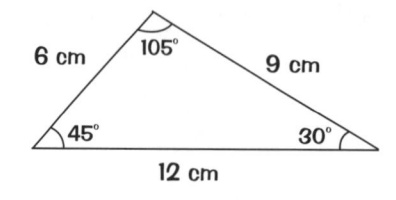

....

Q5 Which of the following must be **similar** to each other? Circle any correct answers.

    A Two circles   **C** Two rectangles   **E** Two equilateral triangles
    B Two rhombuses   **D** Two squares   **F** Two isosceles triangles

SECTION TWO — SHAPES AND AREA

Section Three — Measurements

Metric and Imperial Units

Make sure you know how to change between different metric units. You usually have to multiply or divide by 10, 100 or 1000.

Q1 Fill in the gaps to show how to change between **metric units**:

1 cm = ... mm   1 m = ... cm   1 km = ... m

1 kg = ... g   1 tonne = ... kg   1 litre = ... ml

Q2 Change each of the weights below from kg to **g**.

5 kg = ... g   2.5 kg = ... g   0.7 kg = ... g

Change each of the weights below from g to **kg**.

3000 g = ... kg   4300 g = ... kg   600 g = ... kg

Q3 Change the measurements of the pencil and notebook to **centimetres** (cm).

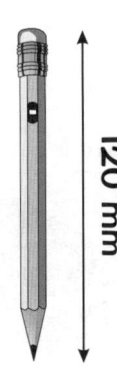

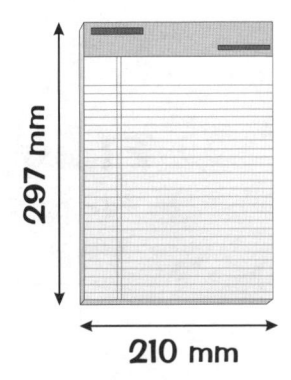

120 mm = ... cm

210 mm = ... cm

297 mm = ... cm

Q4 Jeff's jug has a scale in litres, but he wants to mark on the amounts in **millilitres** (ml).

Fill in the missing values on the jug.

One has been done for you.

1.5 .... ml

1 — 1000 ml

0.5 .... ml

Metric and Imperial Units

Use this information to help with this page.

IMPERIAL UNIT CONVERSIONS

1 foot = 12 inches   1 yard = 3 feet   1 gallon = 8 pints

1 stone = 14 pounds (lbs)   1 pound = 16 ounces (oz)

Q5 Change each of the weights below from stones to **pounds** (lbs).

10 stone = ... lbs   5 stone = ... lbs   3 stone = ... lbs

Change each of the amounts below from gallons to **pints**.

5 gallons = ... pints   20 gallons = ... pints   40 gallons = ... pints

Q6 Change the weights of the cake ingredients below from ounces (oz) to **pounds** (lbs).

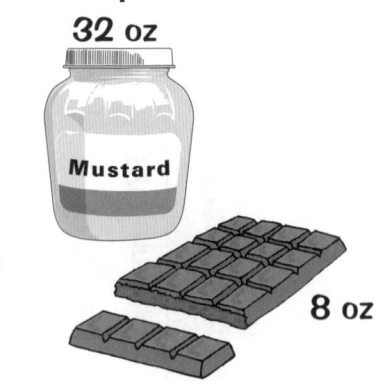

48 oz = ... lbs

32 oz = ... lbs

8 oz = ... lbs

Q7 Fill in the **missing values** in the table.

	Length in Inches	Length in Feet	Length in Yards
	72	6	2
a)	36		1
b)	360	30	
c)		9	3
d)	18		0.5
e)	180	15	

E.g. 72 inches
= 6 feet
= 2 yards.

Section Three — Measurements

Conversion Factors

Here's the method for conversion questions:

1) Find the Conversion Factor
2) Multiply by it AND divide by it
3) Choose the common sense answer

The conversion factor is the link between the two things — e.g. there are 100 cm in 1 m so the conversion factor is 100.

Q1 Fill in the gaps below using the conversion factors for **metric units**:

20 mm = ... cm   6 cm = ... mm   3000 m = ... km

.... m = 2 km   4 km = ... m   .... mm = 3 cm

8000 g = ... kg   2 l = ... ml   4000 ml = ... l

Q2 Justin is shopping on a US website.

Use this exchange rate ⟶ $\boxed{1.60 \text{ US Dollars (\$)} = £1.}$
to calculate the **cost in pounds** (£) of:

a) A book costing $16

.... = £ ....

b) An MP3 player costing $104

.... = £ ....

c) An electric guitar costing $848

.... = £ ....

d) Justin needs to get his things posted from the US to the UK.
A US company charges $160 and a UK company charges £90.
Which company is **cheaper** to use?

....

Q3 Jeremy's car has a 1.4 litre engine.

How big is the engine in **millilitres** (ml)?

.... ml

Q4 Chris wants to paint a table, which has an area of **1000 cm²**.

Find the area of the table surface in **m²** (conversion factor is 1 m² = 10 000 cm²).

.... m²

SECTION THREE — MEASUREMENTS

Rounding Off

Q1 Round the following to the nearest **whole number**:

a) 2.9 .... b) 26.8 .... c) 2.2 ....

d) 11.1 .... e) 6.3 .... f) 43.5 ....

g) 9.9 .... h) 0.4 ....

Think about what two whole numbers each one lies between, and pick the one that it's nearest to.

Q2 An average family has **2.3 children**. How many children is this to the nearest **whole number**?

....

Q3 By the time she is 25 the average woman will have driven **4.72 cars**. What is this to the nearest **whole number**?

....

Q4 Give these amounts to the nearest **pound**:

a) £4.29 .... b) £16.78 .... c) £12.06 ....

d) £7.52 .... e) £0.93 .... f) £14.50 ....

g) £7.49 .... h) £0.28 ....

Q5 Give these measurements to the nearest **whole number**:

a) 2.75 m .... m b) 3.6 miles .... miles

c) 8.3 kg .... kg d) 245.2 s .... s

e) 0.7 cm .... cm f) 190.9 ml .... ml

Section Three — Measurements

Rounding Off

Q6 Round off these numbers to the **nearest 10**:

a) 23 ....   b) 78 ....   c) 65 ....   d) 99 ....

e) 118 ....   f) 243 ....   g) 958 ....   h) 1056 ....

Q7 Round off these numbers to the **nearest 100**:

a) 627 ....   b) 791 ....   c) 199 ....   d) 450 ....

e) 1288 ....   f) 3329 ....   g) 2993 ....

Q8 Round off these football crowd sizes to the **nearest 1000**:

a) 23 324 ....

b) 36 844 ....

c) 49 752 ....

Q9 Round off these numbers to **1 decimal place** (1 d.p.):

a) 7.34 ....   b) 8.47 ....   c) 12.08 ....   d) 28.03 ....

e) 9.35 ....   f) 14.62 ....   g) 30.41 ....

Q10 The number of drawing pins in the box has been rounded to the **nearest 10**.

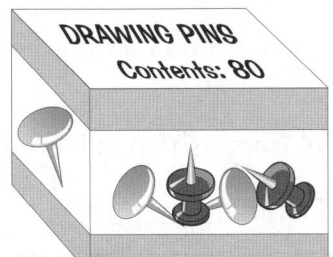

DRAWING PINS
Contents: 80

a) What is the **smallest** number of drawing pins that could be in the box?

....

b) What is the **biggest** number of drawing pins that could be in the box?

....

Think what the smallest number is that would be rounded up to 80. Then think what the biggest number is that would be rounded down.

If a number has been rounded off, the ACTUAL number could be **bigger** or smaller...

SECTION THREE — MEASUREMENTS

Clock Time Questions

You need to know the difference between 12 hour clock and 24 hour clock. Here's a little reminder...

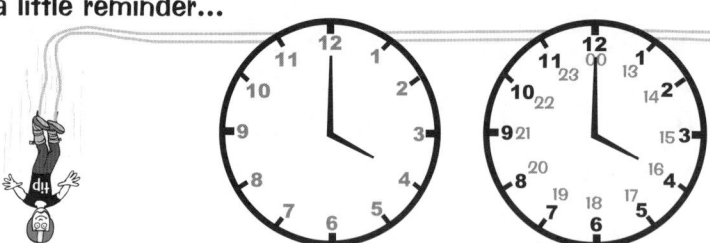

Q1 The times below are given in 24 hour clock.
Using am or pm, give each time in **12 hour clock**.

a) 0400 ....   b) 0215 ....   c) 2130 ....

Q2 The times below are in 12 hour clock. Give each time in **24 hour clock**.

a) 11.22 am ....   b) 12.30 pm ....   c) 3.33 pm ....

Q3 Change the following times from hours into **minutes**:

a) 0.75 hours ....   b) 0.2 hours ....   c) 1.5 hours ....

Q4 Fran is going to cook a ham. The ham needs to be cooked for **245 minutes**.
Fran puts the ham in the oven at **11.55 am**. What time will it be ready?

....

Q5 Steve sets off on a bike ride at **10.30 am**. He stops for lunch at **12.15 pm** and sets off again at **1 pm**. He has a **20 minute** rest stop in the afternoon and gets home at **4.50 pm**.

How long did he cycle for altogether? ....

....

Q6 This timetable shows the times of three trains that travel from Asham to Derton.

a) Which train takes the **least time** to go from Asham to Derton? ....

b) Which train takes the **least time** to go from **Cottingham** to Derton?

....

c) I live in Bordhouse.
What is the latest time I can get the train to arrive in Derton **before 2.30 pm**?

Asham – Derton	Train 1	Train 2	Train 3
Asham	0832	1135	1336
Bordhouse	0914	1216	1414
Cottingham	1002	1259	1456
Derton	1101	1404	1602

....

Section Three — Measurements

Compass Directions and Bearings

Q1 Start at the **dot** on the grid and follow the **directions**, drawing straight lines as you go.

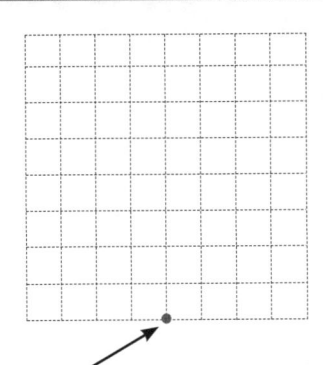

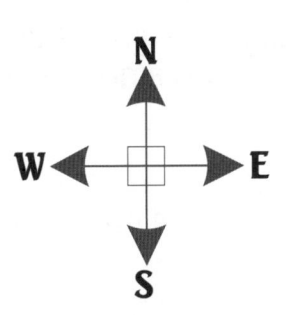

a) West 4 squares.
b) North 4 squares.
c) East 4 squares.
d) South 4 squares.
e) North East through 2 squares.
f) North 4 squares.
g) South West through 2 squares.
h) West 4 squares.
i) North East through 2 squares.
j) East 4 squares.

What **shape** have you drawn? ....

Q2

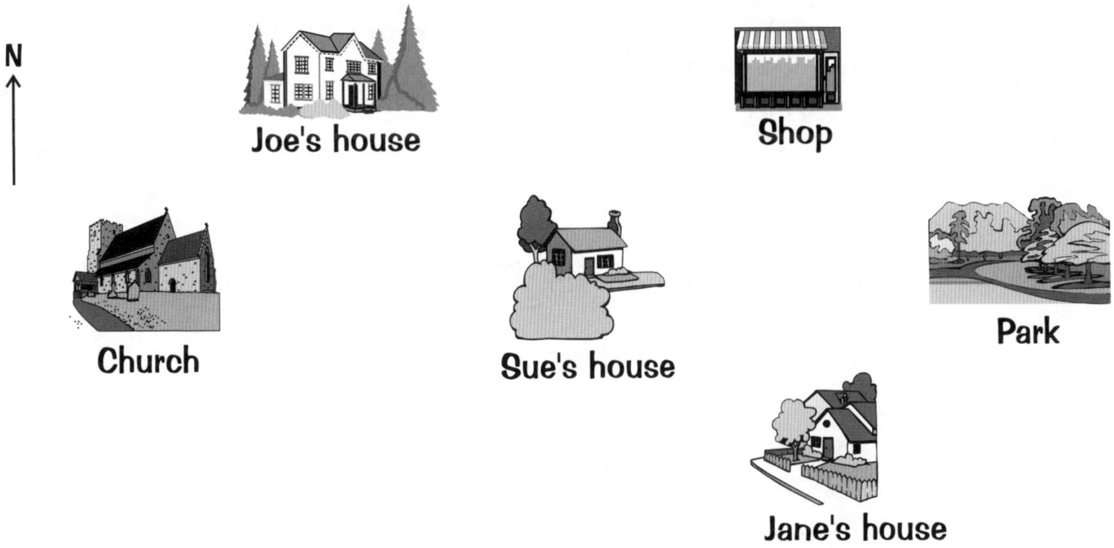

a) What direction does **Jane** go to get to **Sue's house**? ....

b) What direction is the **church** from **Joe's house**? ....

c) What is **South East** of **Sue's house**? ....

d) What is **West** of **Sue's house**? ....

e) Jane is at home. She is going to the **park** first, then the **shop**, and then to **Joe's house**. Write down Jane's directions.

....

You could use "Naughty Elephants Squirt Water" to remember the compass points, but it's more fun to make one up — like Not Everyone Squeezes Wombats... (hmm)

SECTION THREE — MEASUREMENTS

Compass Directions and Bearings

Bearings always have three digits.
So if you've measured 60°, you write it as 060°.

This is a map of a town near the sea.
1 cm on the map is **1 km** in real life.

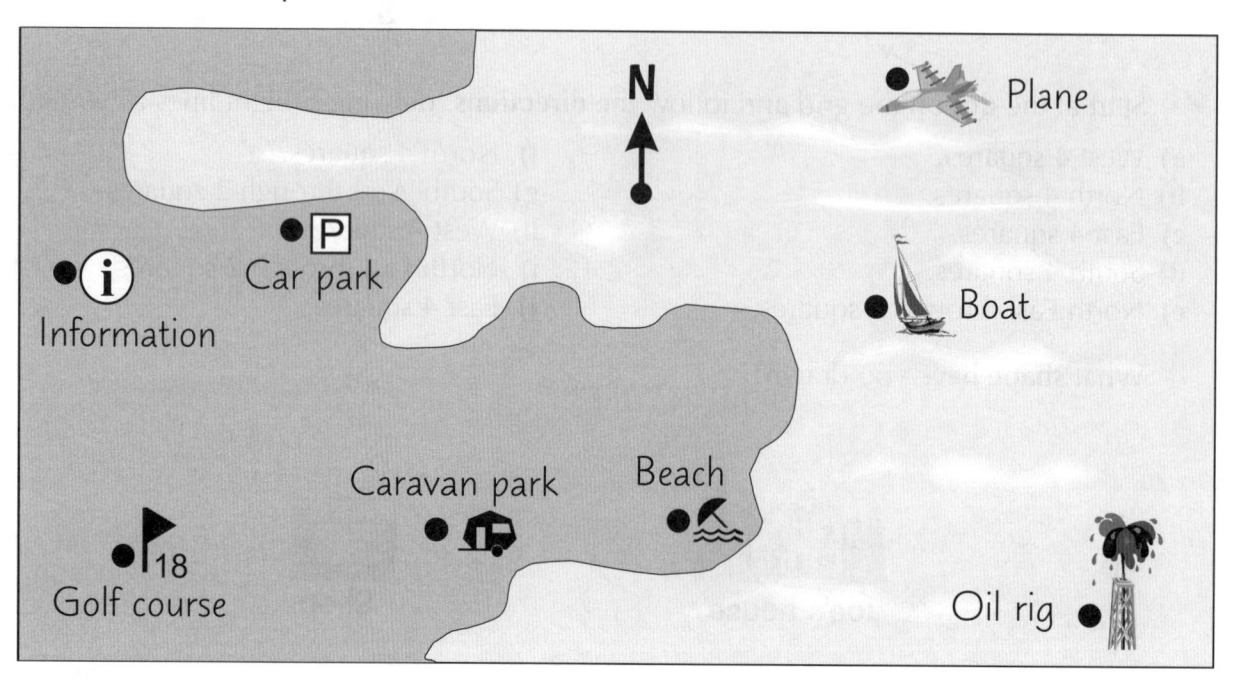

Q3 What is the **bearing** of the caravan park from the tourist information?

....

Q4 What is the **bearing** of the car park from the beach?

....

Q5 **How far** and on what **bearing** is:

	Distance in km	Bearing
a) The boat **from** the plane?	....	....
b) The boat **from** the oil rig?	....	....
c) The plane **from** the oil rig?	....	....

Q6 Mark on the map the point at a bearing of **050°** from the golf course, at a distance of **4.5 km** away from it. Put a ☆ at this point.

Do the direction bit first — and draw a straight line. Then measure the correct distance along it.

SECTION THREE — MEASUREMENTS

Maps and Map Scales

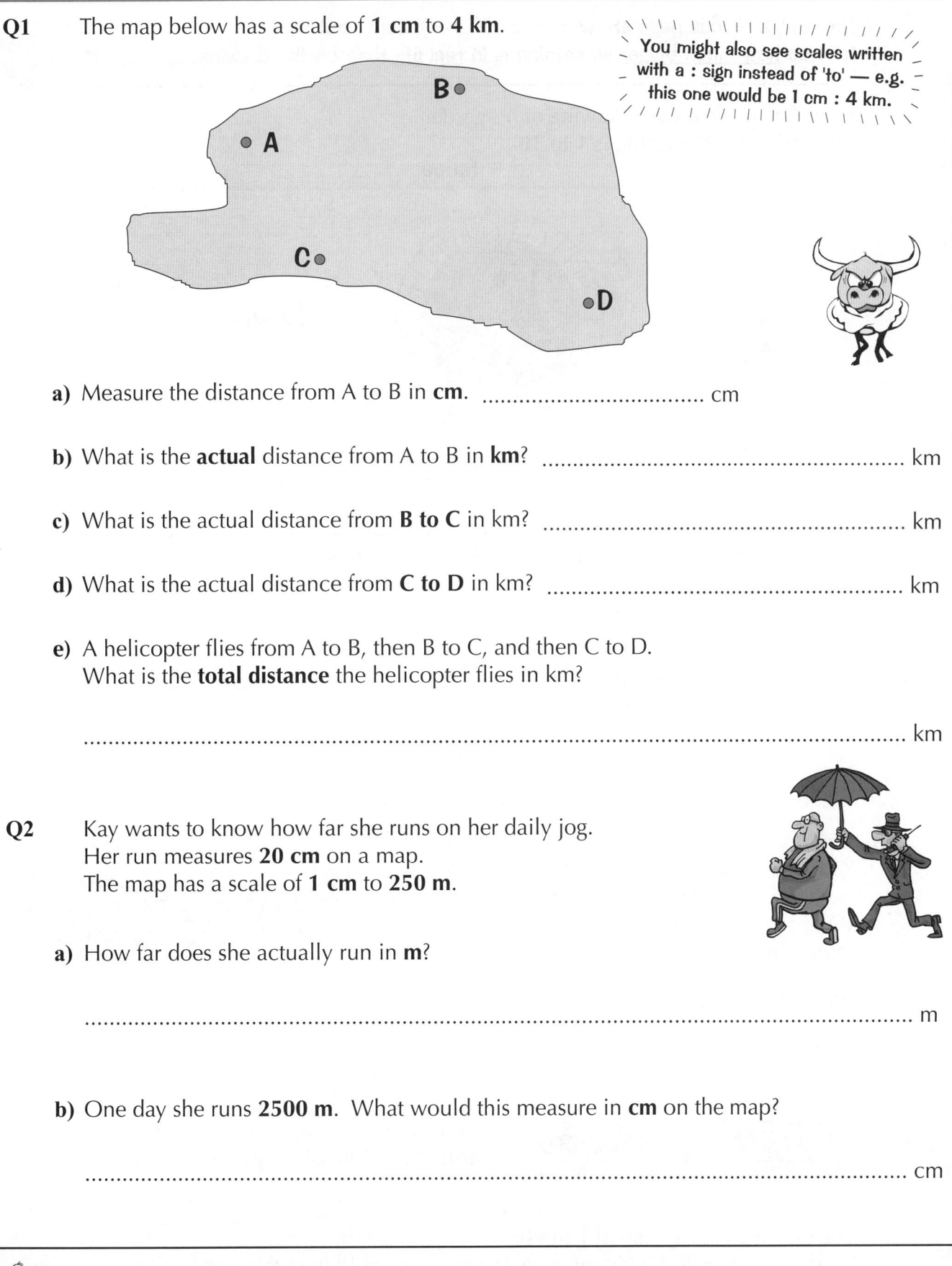

Q1 The map below has a scale of **1 cm** to **4 km**.

You might also see scales written with a : sign instead of 'to' — e.g. this one would be 1 cm : 4 km.

a) Measure the distance from A to B in **cm**. .... cm

b) What is the **actual** distance from A to B in **km**? .... km

c) What is the actual distance from **B to C** in km? .... km

d) What is the actual distance from **C to D** in km? .... km

e) A helicopter flies from A to B, then B to C, and then C to D. What is the **total distance** the helicopter flies in km?

.... km

Q2 Kay wants to know how far she runs on her daily jog. Her run measures **20 cm** on a map. The map has a scale of **1 cm** to **250 m**.

a) How far does she actually run in **m**?

.... m

b) One day she runs **2500 m**. What would this measure in **cm** on the map?

.... cm

If the scale doesn't say what units it's in, it just means that both bits are the same units — so 1 to 1000 could mean 1 cm to 1000 cm, or 1 mm to 1000 mm, etc.

SECTION THREE — MEASUREMENTS

Maps and Map Scales

The scales on this page are written in different ways, but they all tell you <u>how much bigger</u> something is in <u>real life</u> than on the drawing.

Q3 Frank has made a scale drawing of his garden.
The scale on the drawing is **1 to 50**.

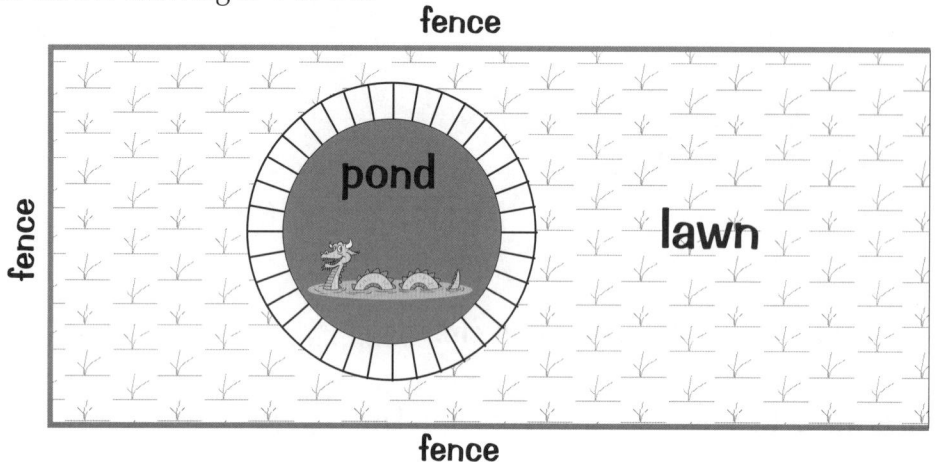

Frank wants to put a fence around the **three outside edges** of the lawn, as shown.
What is the **actual distance** around the three edges in **cm**?

.... cm

Q4 A room measures 20 m long and 16 m wide. Work out the measurements for a scale drawing of the room using a scale of **1 cm = 2 m**.

Length = ... cm

Width = ... cm

Q5 Katie drew a scale drawing of her computer keyboard. She used a scale of **1:10**.
What are the **actual** measurements of the keyboard?

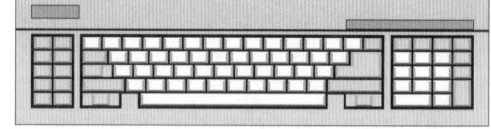

Length = ... cm

Width = ... cm

Q6 This is a scale drawing of part of Paul's kitchen.
Measure the width of the gap for the oven.

.... mm

The drawing uses a scale of **1 to 60**.
Work out the biggest width of oven, in mm, that could fit in the gap.

.... mm

SECTION THREE — MEASUREMENTS

Maps and Directions

There's a great way to remember how to read grid references:
First Across the bottom, Then Up the side. FAT Uncle (or FAT Unicorn, if you like).

Q1 Below is a map of a town centre.

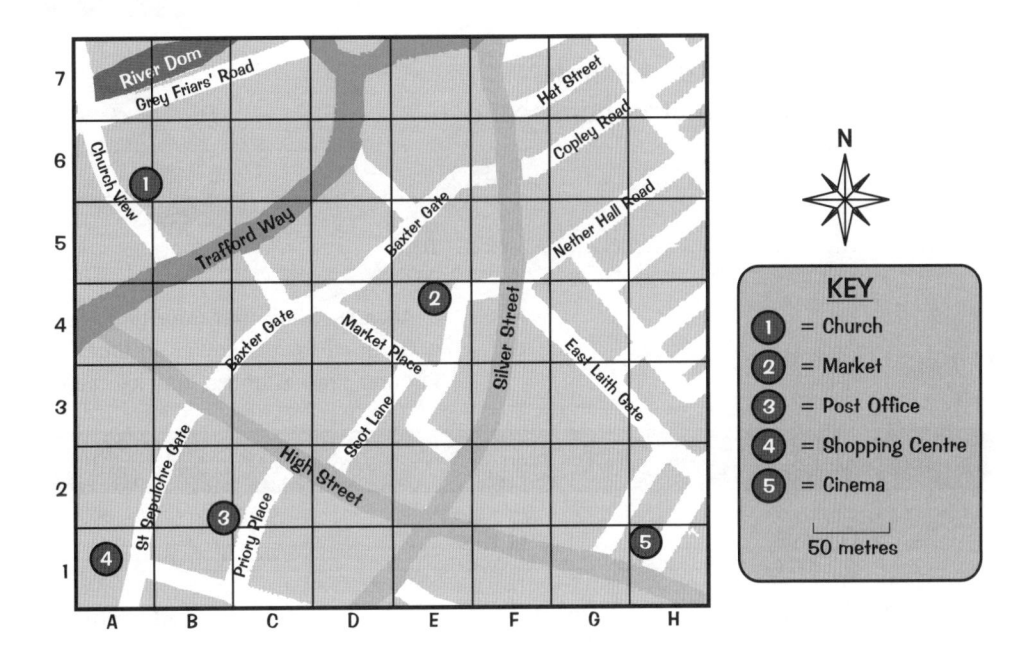

a) What compass direction is the **market from the shopping centre**?

....

b) Ric walks East from the market. When he reaches Silver Street, he walks North East up the street and takes his first left. He then takes his second left.
What **street** is he now standing on?

....

c) Give directions from the **post office** to the **church** by circling the correct words below.

> From the post office head **North East / North West** up Priory Place then
>
> turn **left / right** on to High Street. Take the **first / second** street on the right
>
> on to Trafford Way, then take the first street **left / right** on to Church View.
>
> The church is on the **left / right**.

d) What is the grid reference of the **cinema**? ....

SECTION THREE — MEASUREMENTS

Speed

You need to know the formula for speed, and the formula triangle is useful too.

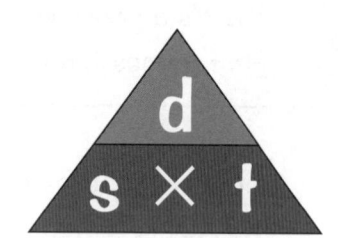

Speed = Distance / Time

Q1 Josh can run **800 m** in **100 seconds**. Calculate his speed in **metres per second** (m/s).

....

.... m/s

Q2 Complete this table:

> Always check that your units for speed match the units used for distance and time. E.g. for distances in km and time in hours, use kilometres per hour (km/h).

Distance	Time	Speed
210 km	3 hrs	.... km/h
135 miles	.... hrs	30 mph
.... km	2.5 hrs	42 km/h
9 miles	0.75 hrs	.... mph
640 km	.... hrs	800 km/h
.... miles	1.25 hrs	60 mph

Q3 A motorbike travels for **3 hours** at a speed of **55 mph**. How far has it travelled in **miles**?

....

.... miles

Q4 Jenny takes **2 hours 30 minutes** to drive **100 km**. What was her speed in **km/h**?

> Work out the time taken in hours first before you use the formula.

....

....

SECTION THREE — MEASUREMENTS

SECTION FOUR — ANGLES AND GEOMETRY

Lines and Angles

Estimating angles is easy once you know the 4 special angles below — then you can compare any other angles to them.

90°   180°   270°   360°

Q1 For each of the angles below write down its **type** and **estimate its size**. The first one has been done for you.

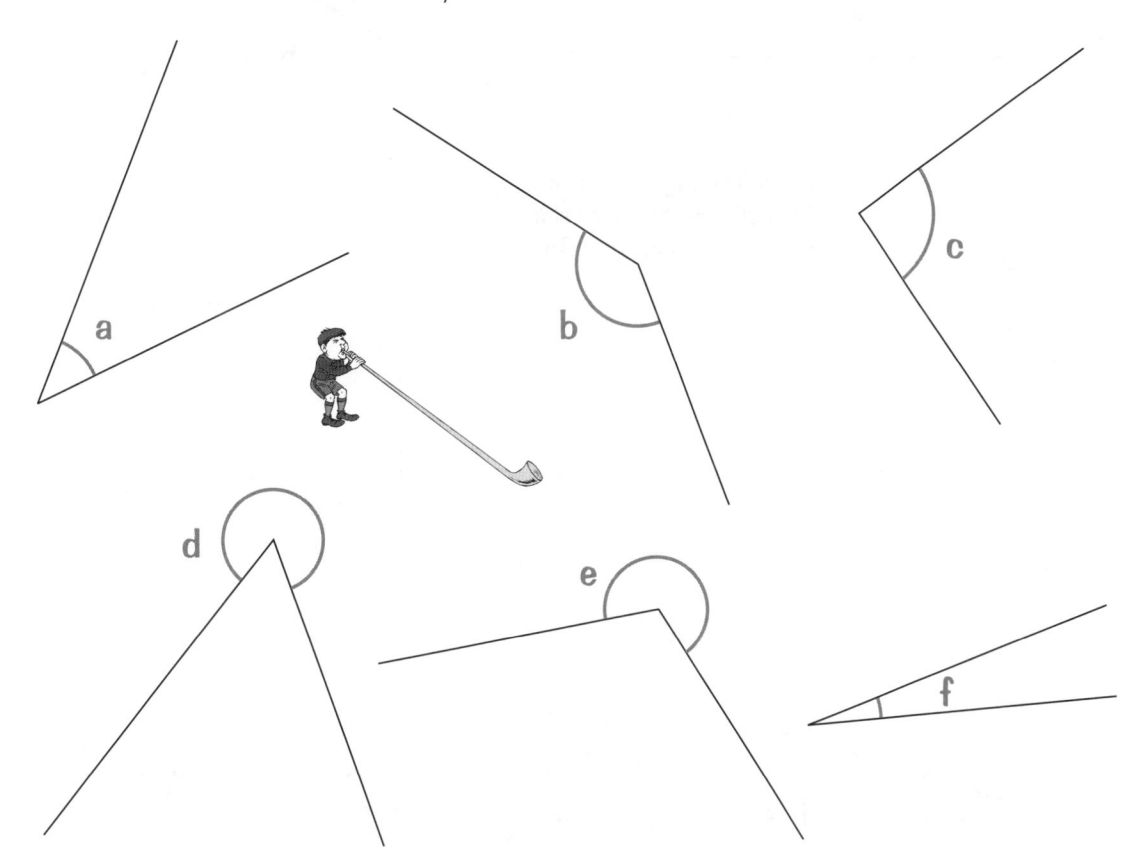

Angle	Type	Estimated Size
a	acute	40°
b	....	....
c	....	....
d	....	....
e	....	....
f	....	....

SECTION FOUR — ANGLES AND GEOMETRY

Measuring Angles with Protractors

It's time to get your protractor out. And remember:
- Put the 0° line at the start of the angle.
- Make sure you read from the right scale.

Q1 Use a **protractor** to **measure** the angles shown:

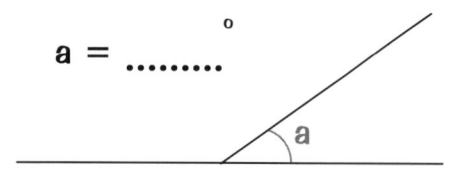

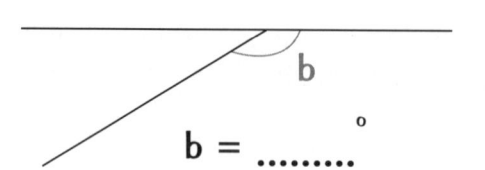

a = ...°

b = ...°

For reflex angles, measure the angle on the other side, then take it away from 360°.

c = ...°

d = ...°

e = ...°

f = ...°

g = ...°

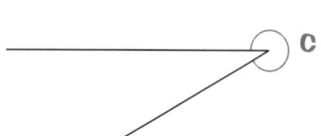

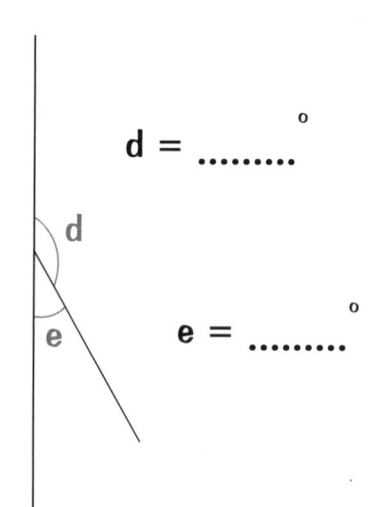

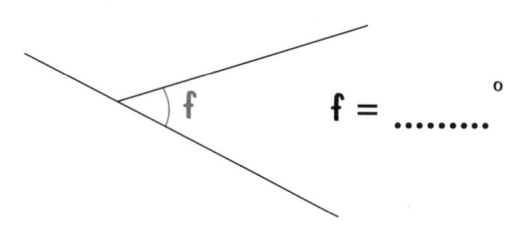

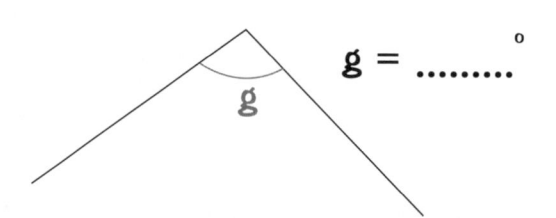

Q2 Use a **protractor** to **measure** the following angles:

a) ABC: ....°

b) BAC: ....°

c) ACB: ....°

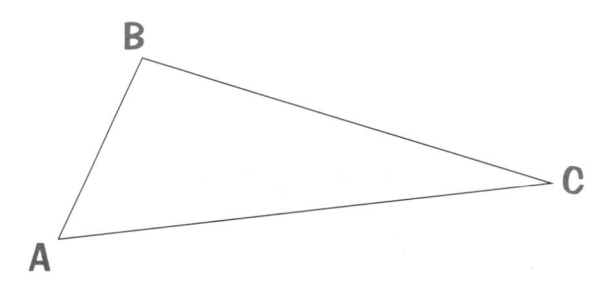

SECTION FOUR — ANGLES AND GEOMETRY

Five Angle Rules

You need to learn the rules for angles on a **straight line** and **round a point**.

Angles on a straight line always add up to 180°

Angles round a point always add up to 360°

Q1 Work out the **angles** labelled below.
They're not drawn to scale so you **shouldn't measure them**.

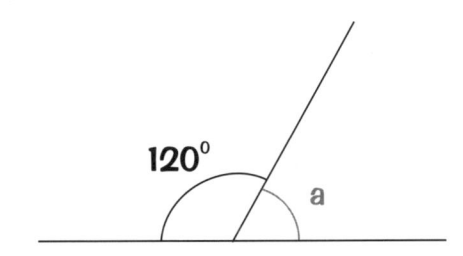

120°   a

b = ...
  = ...°

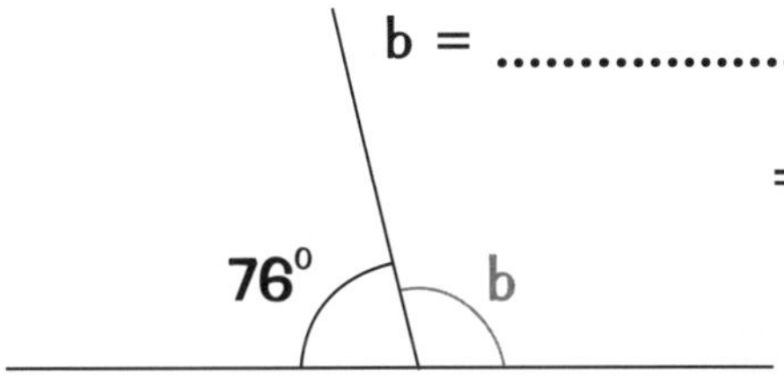

76°   b

a = ...
  = ...°

85°   c

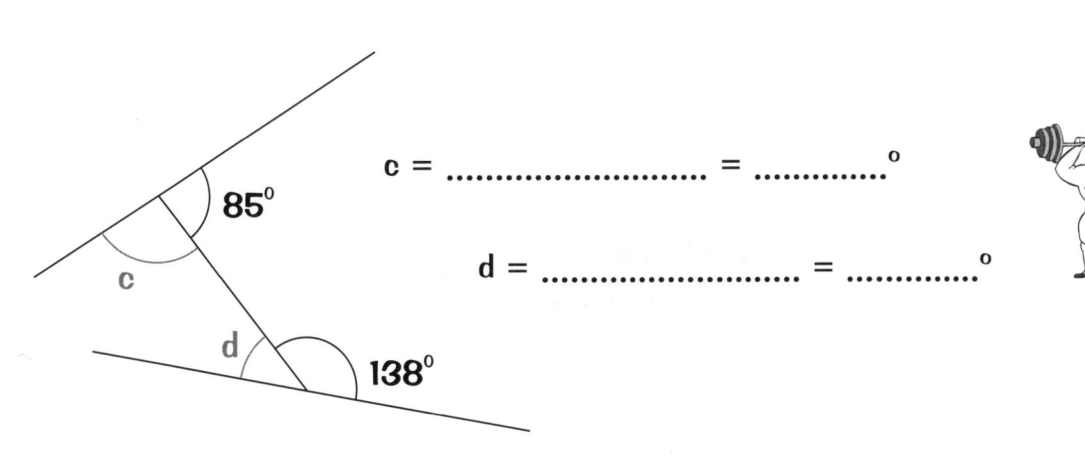

c = ... = ...°

d = ... = ...°

d   138°

e = ... = ...°

f = ... = ...°

g = ... = ...°

e   41°
f   53°
g

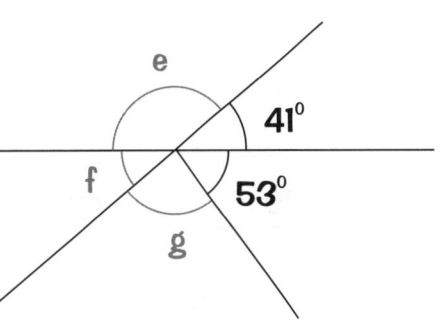

First use the 'angles on a straight line' rule to find e and f, then use the 'angles around a point rule' to find g.

Five Angle Rules

The three angles inside a triangle always add up to 180°

Q2 Work out the missing angle in each of the **triangles** below.
They aren't drawn to scale so you **shouldn't measure them**.

a = ...
 = ...°

(triangle with 40°, 30°, a)

b = ...
 = ...°

(triangle with 35°, 110°, b)

c = ...
 = ...°

(triangle with 79°, 38°, c)

d = ...
 = ...°

(right-angled triangle with 60°, d)

The square means that it's a right angle.

The angles in a quadrilateral always add up to 360°

Q3 Work out the missing angles in these **quadrilaterals**.
They aren't drawn to scale so you **shouldn't measure them**.

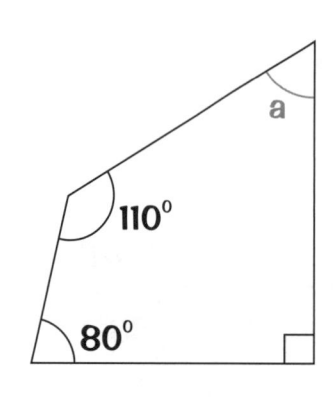

(quadrilateral with 110°, 80°, right angle, a)

a = ...
 = ...°

(kite with 80°, 110°, 110°, b)

b = ...
 = ...°

SECTION FOUR — ANGLES AND GEOMETRY

Five Angle Rules

Isosceles triangles have 2 angles and 2 sides the same.

Q4 Work out the angles labelled a - d in each of these **isosceles triangles**.
They aren't drawn to scale so you **shouldn't measure them**.

a = ...°

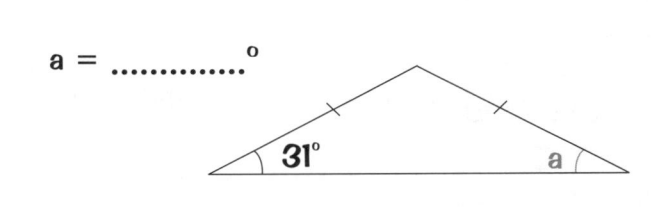

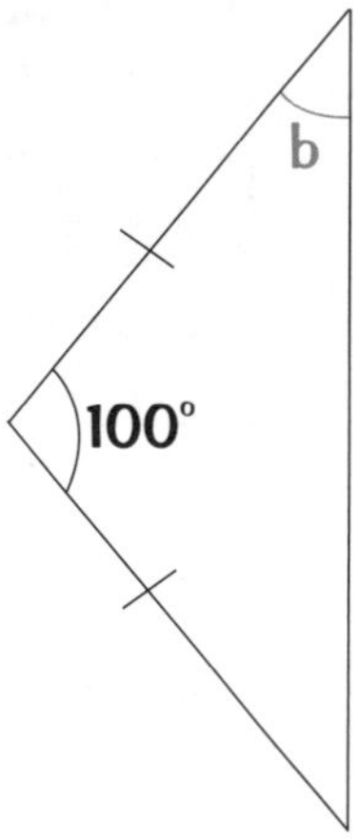

(triangle with 31° and a)

b = ...
....
= ....°

(triangle with 100°)

Think about which 2 angles are the same.

c = ...
....
= ....°

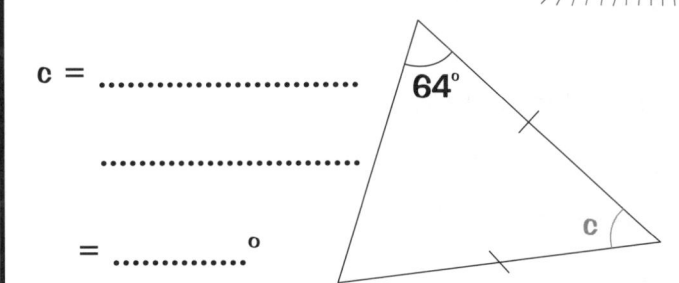

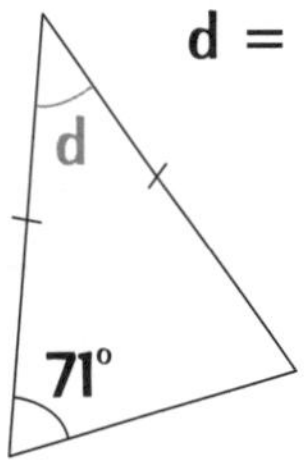

(triangle with 64° and c)

d = ...
....
= ....°

(triangle with 71° and d)

Q5 Two **isosceles triangles** are joined together, as shown.
Work out the angles labelled a - c.

a = ...
= ....°

b = ...
= ....°

c = ...
= ....°

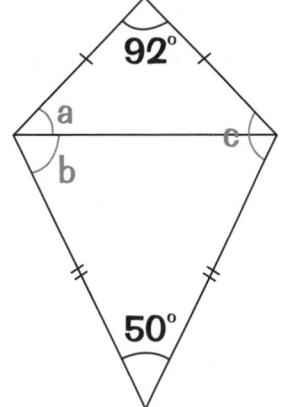

(kite with 92°, a, b, c, 50°)

Use the 'angles in a quadrilateral' rule to find c.

Q6 An **isosceles triangle** has two angles which are **52°** each.
Work out the third angle.

.... = ...°

SECTION FOUR — ANGLES AND GEOMETRY

Parallel and Perpendicular Lines

Once you know the angle rules for parallel lines, you can find all the angles out from just one — ah, such fun...

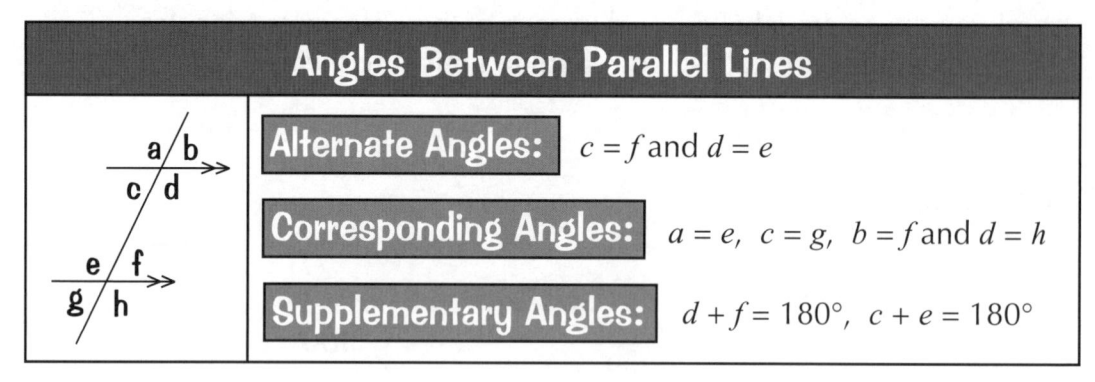

Angles Between Parallel Lines

Alternate Angles: $c = f$ and $d = e$

Corresponding Angles: $a = e$, $c = g$, $b = f$ and $d = h$

Supplementary Angles: $d + f = 180°$, $c + e = 180°$

Q1 a) Lines A and B on the diagram below are **parallel**.
Use the **symbol** for parallel lines to show this on the diagram.

b) Line C is **perpendicular** to A.
Use the **symbol** for perpendicular lines to show this on the diagram.

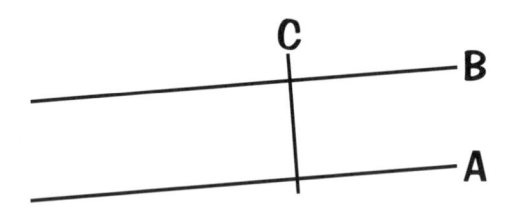

Q2 Find the **sizes** of the angles labelled a and b in the diagrams below.
Write down what **sort of angle** each pair is (alternate, corresponding or supplementary).

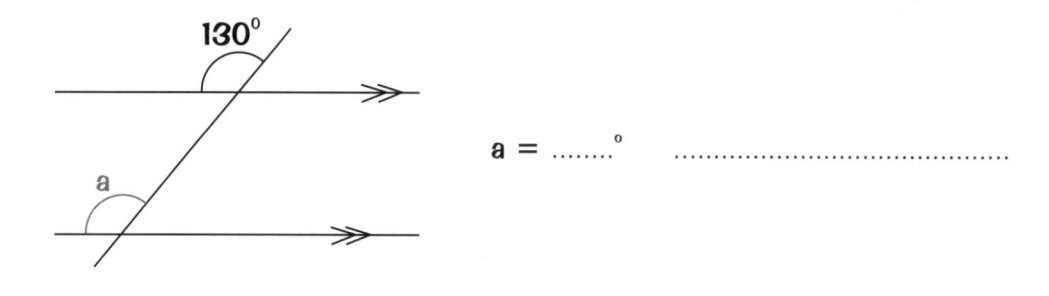

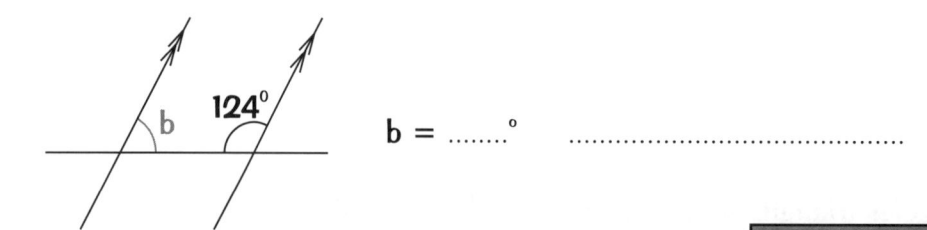

a = ...° ....

b = ...° ....

NOT DRAWN TO SCALE

SECTION FOUR — ANGLES AND GEOMETRY

Parallel and Perpendicular Lines

Q3 Find the **sizes** of the angles labelled c - j in the diagrams below.
Write down what **sort of angle** each pair is (alternate, corresponding or supplementary).

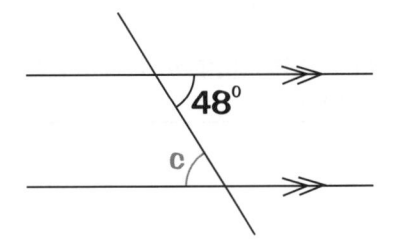

c = ...° ....

d = ...° ....

e = ...° ....

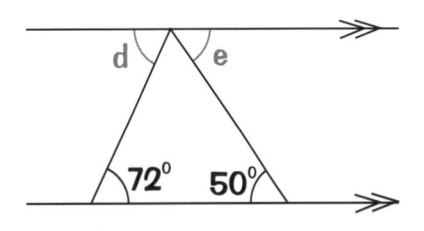

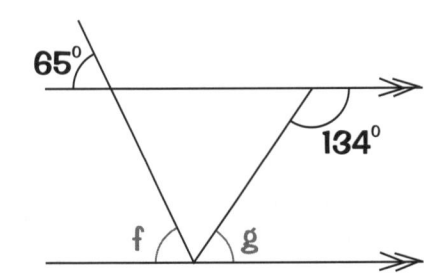

f = ...° ....

g = ...° ....

h = ...° ....

i = ...° ....

j = ...° ....

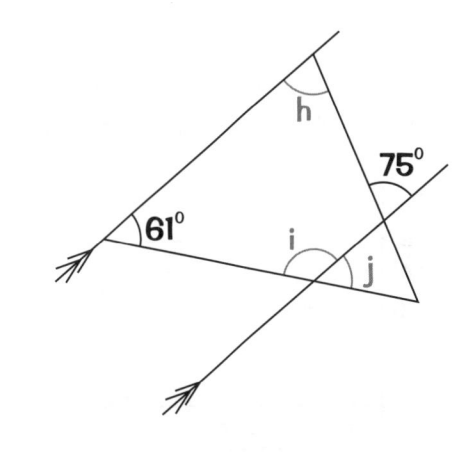

SECTION FOUR — ANGLES AND GEOMETRY

The Four Transformations — Translation

Translations can be written in vector form.

Example: The vector $\binom{2}{5}$ means move 2 spaces to the <u>right</u> and 5 spaces <u>up</u>.

The vector $\binom{-3}{-4}$ means move 3 spaces to the <u>left</u> and 4 spaces <u>down</u>.

Q1 Draw A after the translation $\binom{-4}{-3}$ and label the new shape A′.

Draw B after the translation $\binom{5}{5}$ and label the new shape B′.

Draw C after the translation $\binom{4}{-4}$ and label the new shape C′.

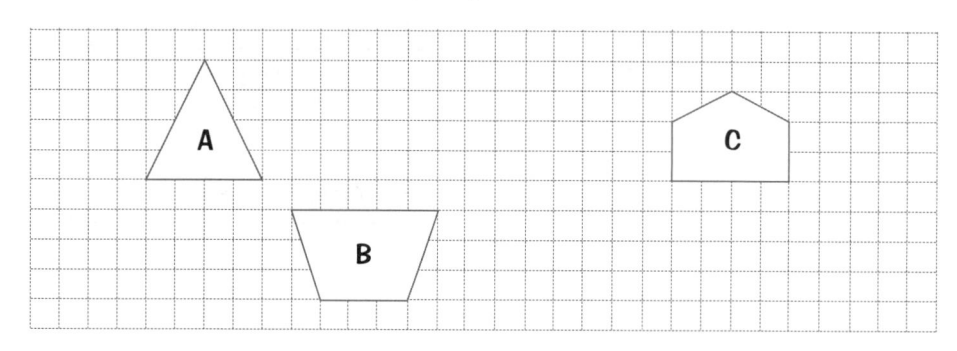

Q2 Translate shape A by the following vectors:

a) $\binom{3}{4}$

b) $\binom{9}{2}$

c) $\binom{3}{-4}$

d) $\binom{-8}{-4}$

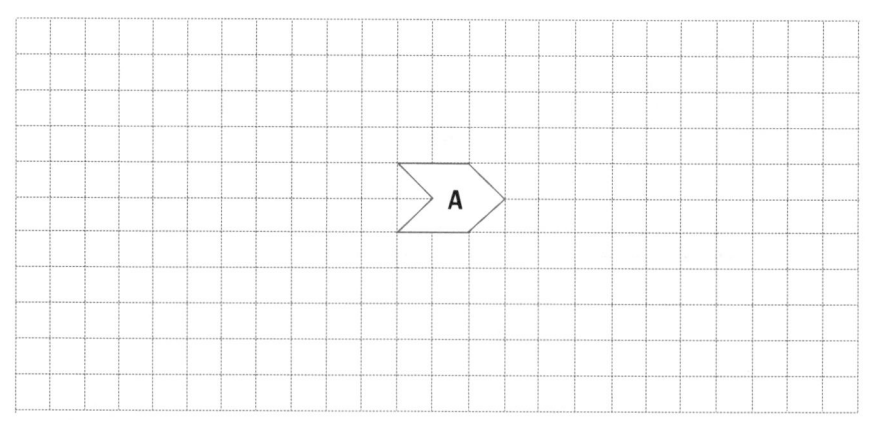

Q3 Write down the **vectors** for the translations shown. The first one has been done for you.

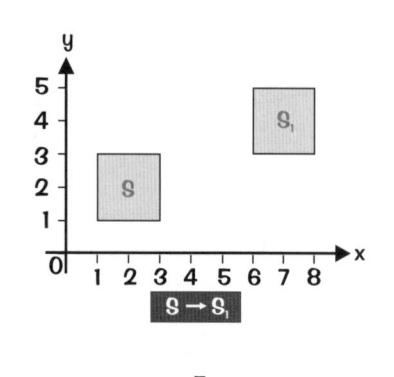

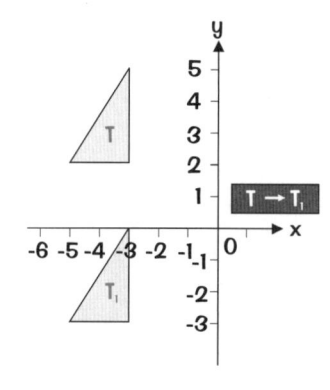

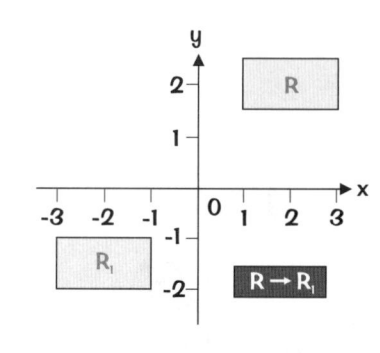

a) $\binom{5}{2}$

b) ....

c) ....

The Four Transformations — Enlargement

The scale factor tells you HOW MUCH BIGGER the enlargement is than the original.

Q1 a) What is the **scale factor** of each of these enlargements?

Just pick one of the sides and see how many times longer it is.

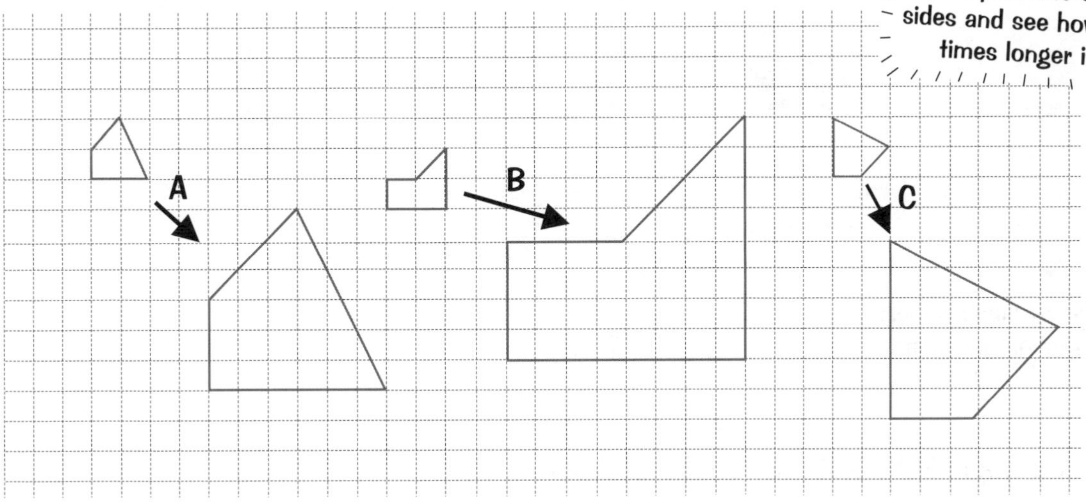

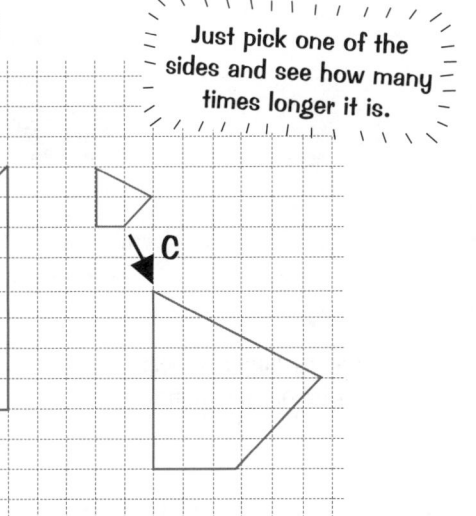

A: Scale factor is .... **B:** Scale factor is .... **C:** Scale factor is ....

b) Mark the **centre of enlargement** on the grid for each of the shapes above.

Q2 Enlarge this triangle using **scale factor 4** anywhere on the grid below.

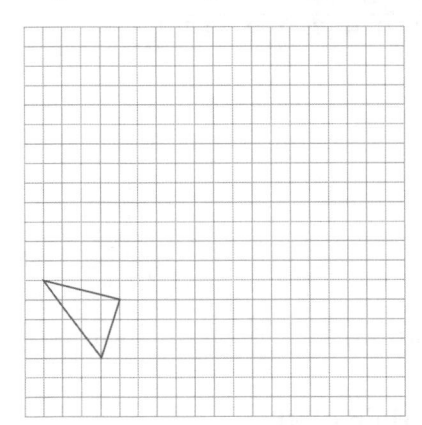

Q3 Enlarge this shape using **scale factor 3** and **centre of enlargement E**.

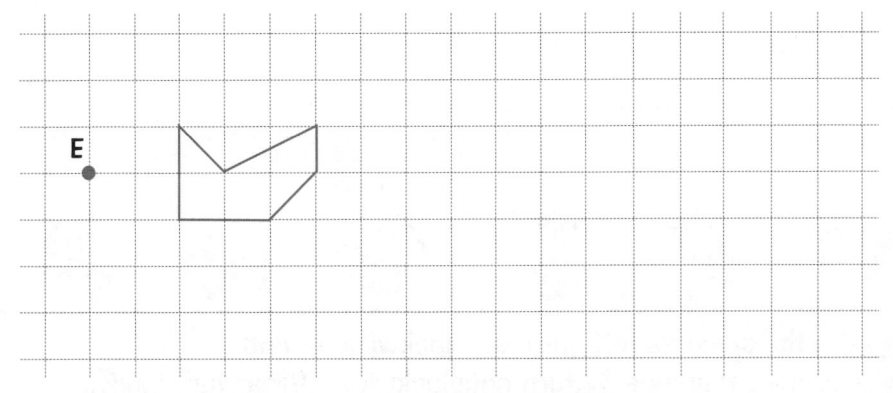

SECTION FOUR — ANGLES AND GEOMETRY

The Four Transformations — Rotation

Q1 The **centre of rotation** for each of these diagrams is the point marked **X**.
Rotate (turn) each shape as asked then draw the **new position** of the shape.

a) 180° (or ½ turn).

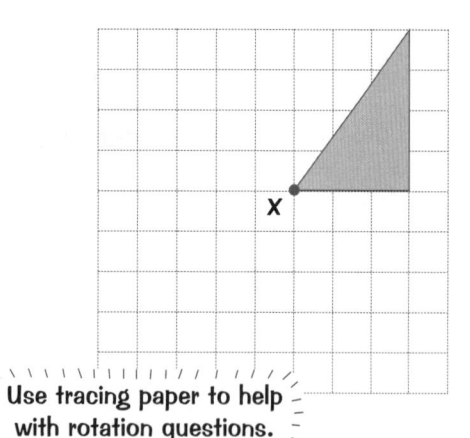

b) 90° clockwise.

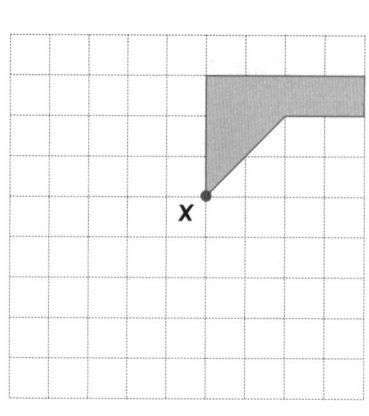

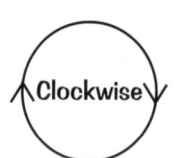

Use tracing paper to help with rotation questions.

Q2 A **triangle** PQR is shown on the grid below.

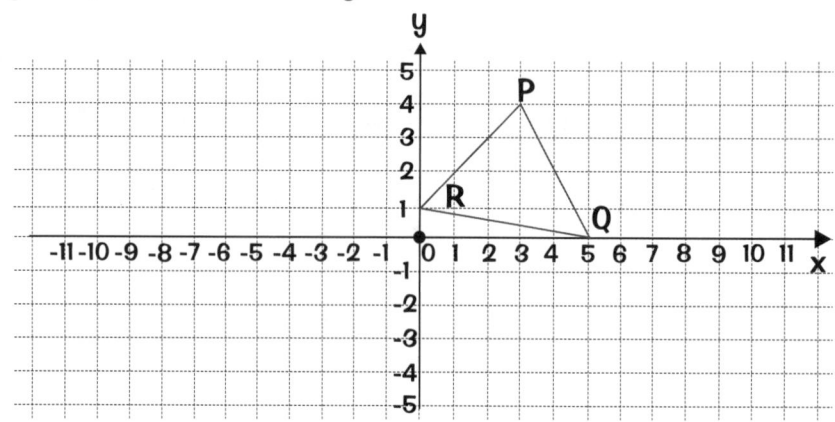

a) Write down the coordinates of:

P .... Q .... R ....

b) Rotate the triangle **90° anticlockwise** about the **origin (0, 0)**.
Label the new triangle P′ Q′ R′.

c) Write down the coordinates of:

P′ .... Q′ .... R′ ....

☞ A ½ turn clockwise is the same as a ½ turn anticlockwise — and a ¼ turn clockwise is the same as a ¾ turn anticlockwise. Great fun, innit...

SECTION FOUR — ANGLES AND GEOMETRY

The Four Transformations — Reflection

Q1 Reflect each shape below in the mirror line.

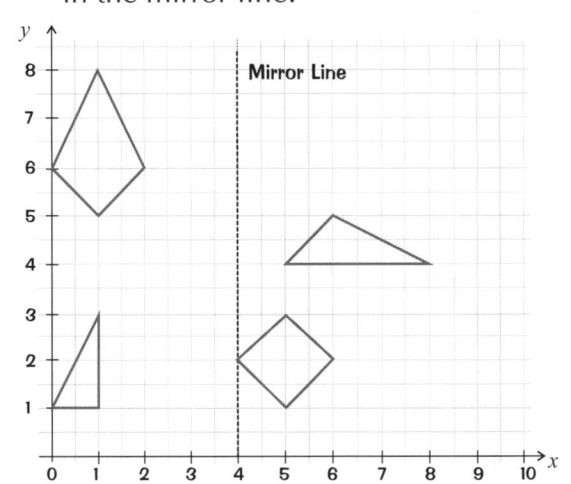

Q2 Reflect each shape below in the mirror line.

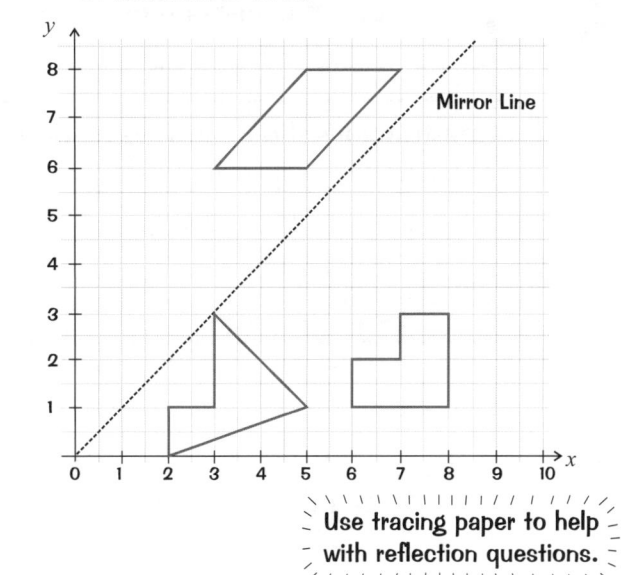

Use tracing paper to help with reflection questions.

Q3 Reflect ① in **mirror line A**, label this ②.

Reflect ② in **mirror line B**, label this ③.

Reflect ③ in **mirror line C**, label this ④.

Reflect ④ in **mirror line D**, label this ⑤.

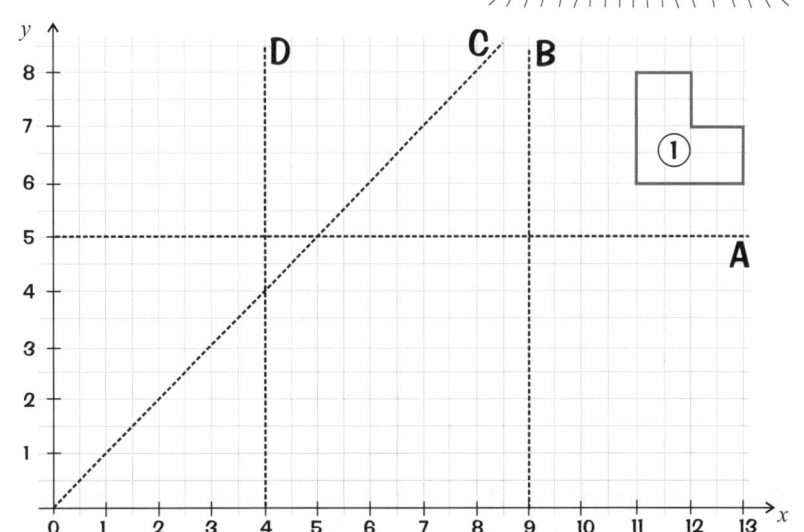

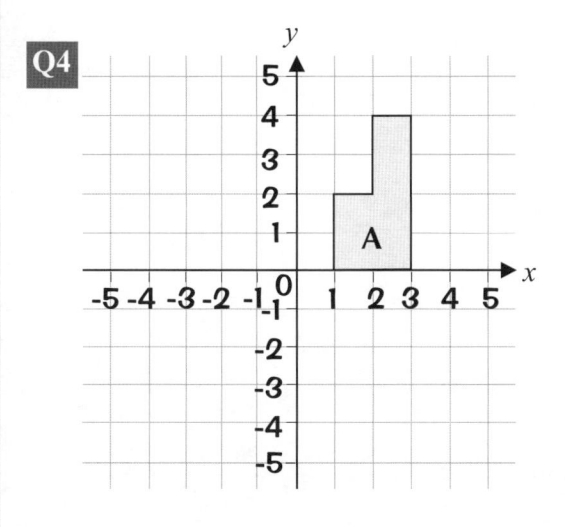

Q4
a) Reflect A in the *x*-axis. Label this A′.
b) Reflect A′ in the *y*-axis. Label this A″.
c) Reflect A″ in the *x*-axis. Label this A‴.
d) What would be the **mirror line** if A was reflected to make A‴?

....

Reflection's just mirror drawing really. And we've all done that before...

SECTION FOUR — ANGLES AND GEOMETRY

Constructing Triangles

**You've got to be really neat with these.
You'll lose marks if your pictures are scruffy.**

Constructions should always be done as accurately as possible using:
- sharp pencil
- ruler
- compasses
- protractor

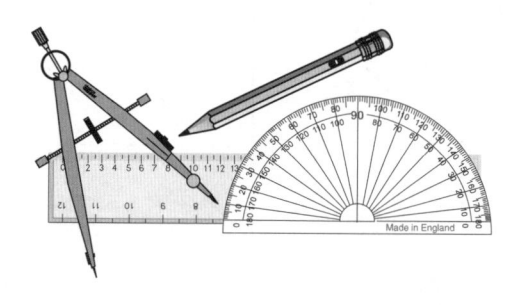

Q1 In the space below, construct a triangle ABC with side lengths
AB = 4 cm, BC = 5 cm, AC = 3 cm.

Leave in your construction lines — don't rub them out.

Q2 In the space below, construct a triangle PQR with side lengths
PQ = 4 cm, QR = 7 cm, PR = 5 cm.

SECTION FOUR — ANGLES AND GEOMETRY

Constructing Triangles

Q3 In the space below, make an accurate drawing of the triangle on the right.

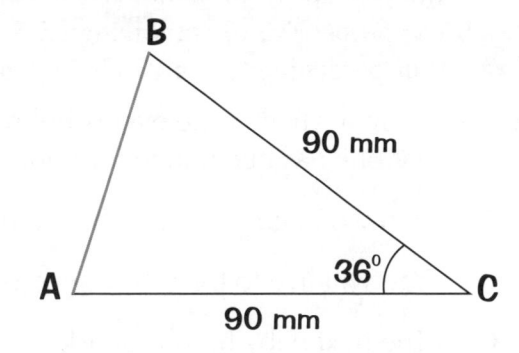

B, 90 mm, A, 90 mm, 36°, C

Measure side **AB** on your triangle. AB = ... mm

Q4 a) In the space below, construct a triangle DEF with **DE = 120 mm**, **DF = 78 mm** and angle **EDF = 70°**.

b) Measure side **EF** on your triangle. EF = ... mm

SECTION FOUR — ANGLES AND GEOMETRY

Probability

The probability of something happening, P, is always between 0 and 1.
The probability of something NOT happening is 1 – P.
(For percentages use 100% instead of 1).

Q1 a) Write down whether the events below are **impossible**, **unlikely**, **even**, **likely** or **certain**. The first one has been done for you.

A — You won't go shopping this month. .... unlikely ....

B — You will live to be 300 years old. ....

C — The next baby born is a girl. ....

D — It will rain this year. ....

b) **Label** the arrows on the probability scale below with letters **A – D** to show the probability of each of the events above. The first one has been done for you.

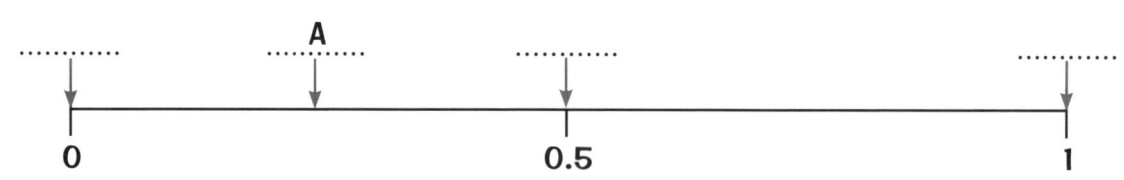

```
     ........        A        ........                        ........
        ↓            ↓            ↓                              ↓
        |————————————|————————————|——————————————————————————————|
        0                        0.5                              1
```

Q2 If the probability of it raining is **75%**, write down the probability of it **not raining**. Give your answer as a percentage.

P(Not rain) = ... %

Q3 There are **two** types of cupcake in a tin — chocolate and lemon. The probability of picking a lemon cake from the tin, P(Lemon) is $\frac{1}{3}$.

Write down the probability of picking a **chocolate cake**. Give your answer as a fraction.

P(Chocolate) = ...

Q4 Mike and Nick play a game. The probability that **Nick will win**, P(Nick), is 0.7.

a) Put an arrow on the scale below to show the probability that **Nick will win**. Label this arrow **N**.

b) If Nick **doesn't** win, then **Mike wins** (there can't be a draw). Work out the probability that **Mike will win**. Give your answer as a decimal.

P(Mike) = ...

c) Put an arrow on the scale to show the probability that **Mike will win**. Label this arrow **M**.

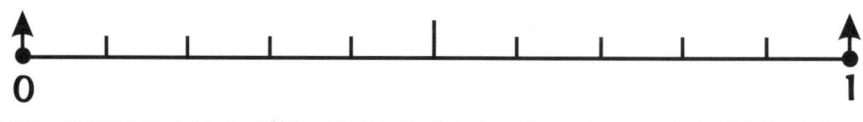

```
        ↑                                                        ↑
        •——|——|——|——|——|——|——|——|——|——•
        0                                                        1
```

Equal and Unequal Probabilities

You can work out probabilities by looking at the total number of different <u>outcomes</u>.

Q1 Write down the probability (as a **fraction**) of the following things happening:

a) A coin landing on tails: P(Tails) = ...

b) A coin landing on heads: P(Heads) = ...

c) A fair, six-sided dice landing on the number 3: P(3) = ...

d) A fair, six-sided dice landing on the number 1: P(1) = ...

Q2 A bag contains **ten balls**.
Five are red, **three** are yellow and **two** are green.
Write down the probability (as a fraction) of picking out:

a) A yellow ball: ....

b) A red ball: ....

c) A green ball: ....

d) A red or a green ball: ....

e) A blue ball: ....

HINT: You need to say how many of that colour there are out of the total number of balls.

Q3 Write down the probability of each of the events below happening.
Write each answer as a **fraction**, as a **decimal** and as a **percentage**.
Example: Tossing a head on a fair coin: ½, 0.5, 50%.

a) Throwing an **odd number** (1, 3 or 5) on a fair, six-sided dice:

Fraction: ...., Decimal: ...., Percentage: .... %

b) Throwing an **even number** (2, 4 or 6) on a fair, six-sided dice:

Fraction: ...., Decimal: ...., Percentage: .... %

c) Picking a **black card** from a standard pack of cards.

Fraction: ...., Decimal: ...., Percentage: .... %

d) Picking a **diamond** from a standard pack of cards.

Fraction: ...., Decimal: ...., Percentage: .... %

There are <u>four types</u> of card in a pack — hearts and diamonds which are red, and clubs and spades which are black. Each type has the same number of cards.

SECTION FIVE — HANDLING DATA

Listing Outcomes

Q1 The **outcome** when you toss a coin is either a head (H) or a tail (T).

a) Fill in the table below to show all the outcomes when two coins are **tossed together**. One has been done for you.

Use the table to answer the following questions:

		2ⁿᵈ COIN	
		H	T
1ˢᵗ COIN	H	H H	
	T		

b) How many possible outcomes are there **in total**? ....

c) Write down the probability of getting **two heads**. ....

d) Write down the probability of getting a **head and a tail**. ....

Q2 Two dice are rolled at the same time and the scores on the dice are **added together**.

a) Complete the table of possible outcomes below, and use it to answer the questions.

b) How many possible outcomes are there in total? ....

		SECOND DICE					
		1	2	3	4	5	6
FIRST DICE	1						
	2	3					
	3						
	4						
	5			8			
	6						

Write down the probability of scoring:

c) 2 ....

d) 6 ....

e) 10 ....

f) More than 9 ....

g) Less than 4 ....

h) More than 12 ....

Q3 The two spinners below are spun and the scores are **added together**.

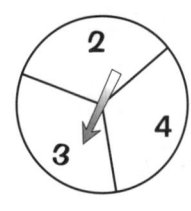

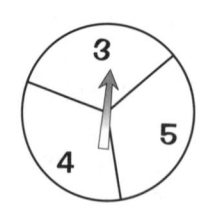

		SPINNER 1		
		2	3	4
SPINNER 2	3			
	4			
	5			

a) Fill in the table of possible outcomes on the right, and use it to answer the questions below.

b) Write down the probability of scoring **7**. ....

c) To win you have to score **8 or more**.
Write down the probability of **winning**. ....

In the exam, you might not be asked to put the "possible outcomes" in a table. But it's a good idea to make a table anyway — that way you don't miss any out.

SECTION FIVE — HANDLING DATA

Types of Data

Q1 Students at a school are doing a project on recycling.
They decide to look up data about recycling on the local council's **website**.

Are the students using **primary** or **secondary** data?

....

Q2 Tick the boxes to show whether the following are **qualitative** or **quantitative** data:

	Qualitative	Quantitative
a) The favourite **foods** of a group of children.	☐	☐
b) The **heights** of people in a show.	☐	☐
c) The **colour** of people's eyes in one family.	☐	☐
d) The length of **time** it takes for a group of runners to each run 100 metres.	☐	☐
e) The **weights** of all the babies born on one day.	☐	☐
f) The favourite **football teams** of a group of friends.	☐	☐

Q3 Fill in the table below to say whether the data is **discrete** or **continuous**.

Data	Discrete or Continuous
Number of people passing through an airport each day.	....
Heights of people in a Maths class.	....
Number of goals scored in a hockey game.	....
Time taken to be served in a fast food restaurant.	....

If you can measure it exactly then it's discrete — otherwise it's continuous.

SECTION FIVE — HANDLING DATA

Samples and Groups

If you are collecting data from a large population, it can be hard to make sense of it all. So it helps to take samples and to put it all in groups.

Q1 Say what the **population** is for each of the surveys below:

a) How smoking affects 20- to 30-year-old women.

....

b) The number of trees in parks in London.

....

c) The pay of football players in the Premier League.

....

Q2 A supermarket wants to find out how to get more customers.
They interview the **first 100 people** to go into their store one Saturday morning.

a) Give one reason why this sample is **biased**.

....

b) What **population** should they have taken a sample from?

....

Q3 Fred asked 30 people the time (in minutes) it took them to eat their dinner.
Here are the results:

```
42  13   6  31  15  20  19   5  50  14
 8  25  16  27   4  45  32  31  31  10
32  17  16  19  29  42  43  30  29  18
```

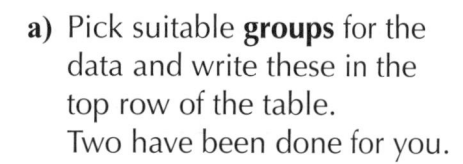

a) Pick suitable **groups** for the data and write these in the top row of the table. Two have been done for you.

Length of time (mins)	1-10	....	....	....	41-50
Number of people	5	....	....	....	....

b) Fill in the bottom row of the table with the **number of people** in each group. One has been done for you.

c) Give one reason why putting data in groups can be a **bad** thing.

....

SECTION FIVE — HANDLING DATA

Questionnaires

Q1 Stanley asks the following question to some students at his school:

How often do you use the school canteen? Tick one of the boxes.

Very often ☐   Quite often ☐   Not very often ☐

a) Write down one thing that is **wrong** with Stanley's question.

....

b) Write a **better question** that Stanley could use to find out how often students at his school use the canteen.

HINT: You might need to have tick boxes.

....

....

Q2 A café owner asks his customers the following question on a questionnaire:

What is your favourite drink?
  i) Tea   ii) Coffee
  iii) Fruit squash   iv) Other

Most people said "**Other**".

a) Write down one thing that is **wrong** with the question.

....

b) How could the café owner **change** the question to make it **better**?

....

Q3 Peter writes a questionnaire about music to give to students at his school. The following question is on the questionnaire:

Do you agree that dubstep is the best type of music? Yes / No.

a) Write down one thing that is **wrong** with Peter's question.

....

b) Write a **better question** that Peter could use to find out what music people like best.

....

....

SECTION FIVE — HANDLING DATA

Questionnaires

Q4 Fill in the blanks below to make a suitable question to find out **how often** people watch TV:

How many days in one week do you watch TV?

a) .... ☐   b) ....1 – 2.............. ☐   c) .... ☐

d) .... ☐   e) ......7................ ☐

Q5 Debby needs to find out **how old people are** in her questionnaire but does not want to offend them.

Fill in the blanks below to make a suitable question for Debby to ask.

How old are you? Please tick one of the boxes below.

a) ....0 – 20.......... ☐   b) .... ☐   c) .... ☐

d) .... ☐   e) .... ☐   f) ......61 +............ ☐

Q6 Frankie wants to find out what snacks people like, so she can serve them at her party. The main choices are **crisps**, **nuts**, **sweets** and **fruit**, or any **other suggestions**.

In the space below, **write a question** that Frankie could write on her party invitations to find out what type of snack people like best. Include **tick boxes** below the question.

....

....

SECTION FIVE — HANDLING DATA

Mode, Median, Mean and Range

To find the mode of a set of numbers, put them in order of size first — then it's easier to see which number you've got most of.

Q1 Find the **mode** for each of the following lists. Put them in order first.

   a) 3, 5, 8, 6, 3, 7, 3, 5, 3, 9

   .... Mode is ....

   b) 52, 26, 13, 52, 31, 12, 26, 13, 52, 87, 41

   .... Mode is ....

Q2 The temperature (in °C) at midday on 10 different days was:

   25, 18, 23, 19, 23, 24, 23, 18, 20, 19

   What was the **modal** temperature?

   .... Modal temperature was ....°C.

Q3 The time (in minutes) it takes thirty pupils in a class to get to school each day is:

   18, 24, 12, 28, 17, 34, 17, 17, 28, 12, 23, 24, 17, 34, 9,
   32, 15, 31, 17, 19, 17, 32, 15, 17, 21, 29, 34, 17, 12, 17

   What is the **modal** time?

   ....

   ....

   Modal time is .... mins.

Put the numbers in size order for median questions too — it makes it easier to find the middle value.

Q4 Find the **median** for the lists below.

   a) 3, 6, 7, 12, 2, 5, 4, 2, 9

   .... Median is ....

   b) 14, 5, 21, 7, 19, 3, 12, 2, 5

   .... Median is ....

Q5 The heights (in cm) of fifteen 16 year olds are listed below.

   162   156   174   148   152   139   167   134
   157   163   149   134   158   172   146

   What is the **median** height? Write your answer in the coloured box.

   Median = ... cm

SECTION FIVE — HANDLING DATA

Mode, Median, Mean and Range

Remember the formula for finding the mean: total of the items ÷ number of items.
The range is the distance from the smallest to the biggest number.

Q6 The number of goals scored by a hockey team over 10 games is listed below.

0, 3, 2, 4, 1, 2, 3, 4, 1, 0

Work out the **range** of the number of goals scored.

.... Range = ...

Q7 Sarah and her friends measured their heights, as listed below:

1.52 m, 1.61 m, 1.49 m, 1.55 m, 1.39 m, 1.56 m

Work out the **range** of the heights.

.... Range = ... m

Q8 Here are the marks of 6 people in a Maths test:

23%, 44%, 15%, 56%, 35%, 7%

a) Work out the **range** of the marks.

.... Range = ...%

b) Work out the **mean** of the marks.

.... Mean = ...%

Q9 Work out the **mean** of each of the lists below.
Round answers to 1 decimal place if you need to.

a) 13, 15, 11, 12, 16, 13, 11, 9 .... Mean = ...

b) 16, 13, 2, 15, 0, 9 .... Mean = ...

c) 80, 70, 80, 50, 60, 70, 90, 60, 50, 70, 70 ....

Mean = ...

Q10 Here are the marks John and Paul got on their last five maths tests.

| John | 65 | 83 | 58 | 79 | 75 |
| Paul | 72 | 70 | 81 | 67 | 70 |

Calculate the **range** for each pupil.

John's Range: ....

Paul's Range: ....

SECTION FIVE — HANDLING DATA

Mode, Median, Mean and Range

Q11 David is on a diet. The table below shows how many calories he ate in a week.
Work out the **mean** and **range** of the number of calories David ate that week.

....

....

Mean = ...   Range = ...

Day	Calories Eaten
Monday	1875
Tuesday	2105
Wednesday	1680
Thursday	1910
Friday	1930

Q12 The shoe sizes in a class of girls are:

3 3 4 4 5 5 5 5 6 6 6 7 8

Find the **mode**, **median**, **mean** and **range** for the shoe sizes.
Round the mean to 1 decimal place if you need to.

Mode = ...   Median = ...

.... Mean = ...

.... Range = ...

Q13 I counted the number of matches in ten matchboxes. These are the results:

241 244 236 240 239 242 237 239 239 236

Find the **mode**, **median**, **mean** and **range** for the number of matches.

.... Mode = ...

.... Median = ...

.... Mean = ...

.... Range = ...

Q14 James measured the heights of a certain type of flower on both sides of the English-Scottish border. The heights are shown below (to the nearest cm).

Scottish side
Heights 14, 15, 17, 14, 17, 16, 14, 13
15, 17, 16, 14, 15, 17, 14, 13

English side
Heights 14, 12, 16, 18, 19, 17, 16, 15
13, 14, 15, 16, 17, 18, 19, 13

a) Find the **median** height of the flowers on the **Scottish** side.

.... Median = ... cm

b) Find the **median** height of the flowers on the **English** side.

.... Median = ... cm

c) On which side are you likely to see **taller** flowers?

....

SECTION FIVE — HANDLING DATA

Frequency Tables

Q1 At a car show, 60 people were asked what car they drove.
Jeremy wrote down the results using the code below.

Saloon - S   Hatchback - H   4 × 4 - F   MPV - M   Roadster - R

Here is the full list of results:

H	S	R	S	S	R	M	F	S	S	R	R
M	H	S	H	R	H	M	S	F	S	M	S
R	R	H	H	H	S	M	S	S	R	H	H
H	H	R	R	S	S	M	M	R	H	M	H
H	S	R	F	F	R	F	S	M	S	H	F

a) Use the list of results to fill in the table below, and add up the **frequency** in each row.

TYPE OF CAR	TALLY	FREQUENCY
Saloon		
Hatchback		
4 × 4		
MPV		
Roadster		

The modal car is the one that has the highest frequency — it's the most common.

b) What is the **modal** type of car? ....

Q2 Last season Newcaster City played 32 matches.
The number of goals they scored in each match are shown below.

```
2  4  3  5          1  0  0  1
1  0  3  2          1  1  1  0
4  2  1  2          1  3  2  0
0  2  3  1          1  1  0  4
```

a) Use the list above to complete the **frequency table** below.

GOALS	TALLY	FREQUENCY
0		
1		
2		
3		
4		
5		

b) Work out the **range** of goals scored.

....

c) What was the **modal** number of goals scored?

....

SECTION FIVE — HANDLING DATA

Finding The Mean From Frequency Tables

Q1 A tornado has hit a village. Many houses have had windows broken. The frequency table below shows the effects of the tornado in the village.

No. of windows broken per house	0	1	2	3	4	5	6	Totals
Frequency	5	3	4	11	13	7	2	
Windows × Frequency								

a) What is the **modal** number of broken windows? ....

b) Work out the **range** of broken windows. ....

c) **Complete** the frequency table by working out the values for the third row, and adding up the totals.

d) Use the table to find the **mean** number of broken windows. Round your answer to 1 decimal place if you need to.

.... Mean = ...

Q2 The frequency table below shows the **number of hours** spent Christmas shopping by **100 people** in a town centre.

Number of Hours	0	1	2	3	4	5	6	7	8
Frequency	1	9	10	10	11	27	9	15	8
Hours × Frequency									

a) What is the **modal** number of hours spent Christmas shopping? ....

b) Fill in the **third row** of the table.

c) Work out the **total amount of time** spent Christmas shopping by all 100 people.

The total time is the total of the third row of the table.

....

d) Use the table to find the **mean** number of hours spent Christmas shopping.

.... Mean = ... hours

SECTION FIVE — *HANDLING DATA*

Line Graphs and Pictograms

To draw line graphs — just plot the points, then join them up with straight lines.

Q1 Billy took his temperature every hour and recorded it on the **line graph** below.

Use the graph to answer the following questions:

a) What was his temperature at **10am**?

.... °C

b) What was his temperature at **2pm**?

.... °C

c) What was his **highest** temperature?

.... °C

d) **When** was his temperature highest?

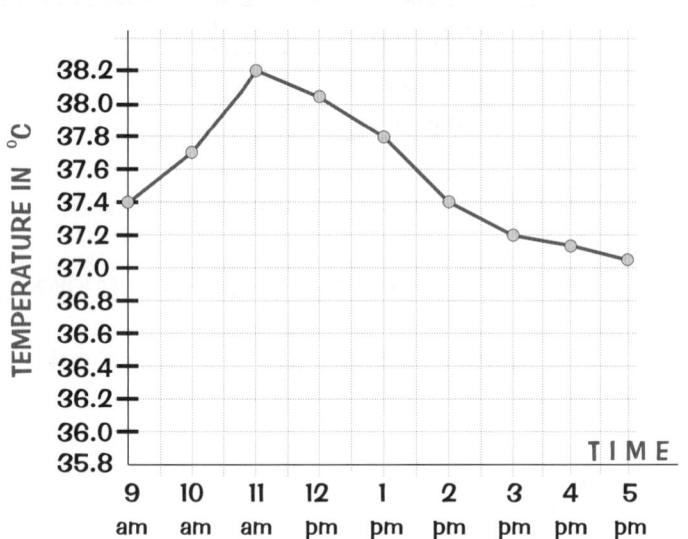

....

Q2 David weighed himself every 5 days. The results are given in the table below. Use the table to **draw a line graph** to show how David's weight changed.

DAY	0	5	10	15	20	25	30
WEIGHT (KG)	88.9	88.4	87.6	87.5	87.5	87.2	87.0

In your own words, **describe** how David's weight changed:

....
....
....
....
....

SECTION FIVE — HANDLING DATA

Line Graphs and Pictograms

Pictograms use a picture to stand for a certain amount of things or people. There should always be a <u>key</u> to tell you <u>how many</u> the picture represents.

Q3 Mary asked 50 people what musical instrument they could play.

> **25** could **not** play an instrument, **10** could play the **piano**, **10** could play the **guitar**, and **5** could play the **banjo**.

Use this information to complete the pictogram below.

♫ Means 5 people.

Instrument	Number of People
None	
Piano	
Guitar	
Banjo	♫

Q4 This pictogram shows the favourite drinks of a group of pupils.

Favourite Drinks	Number of Pupils
Lemonade	✧ ✧ ✧ ✧ ✧ ✧ ✧ ✧ ✧
Cola	✧ ✧ ✧ ✧ ✧ ✧ ✧ ✧ ✧ ✧
Cherryade	✧ ✧ ✧ ✧ ✧ ✧
Orange Squash	✧ ✧ ✧
Milk	✧

✧ Means **2 pupils**.

a) How many pupils liked **orange squash** best?

.... pupils.

b) 18 pupils liked lemonade best. Work out how many **more** liked cola best.

.... pupils.

c) Work out how many **more** pupils liked cola best compared with milk.

.... pupils.

d) How many pupils were asked **in total**?

.... pupils.

SECTION FIVE — HANDLING DATA

Two-Way Tables

Q1 Fill in the spaces to complete the two-way table below.

	Male	Female	Total
Can Drive	37	41	....
Can't Drive	15	7	....
Total	....	....	....

Q2 Fill in the spaces to complete the two-way table below.

	Aged under 20	Aged 20+	Total
Vegetarian	3	....	7
Not Vegetarian	....	11	....
Total	....	....	30

Q3 The two-way table below shows the type of vehicles recorded on a stretch of road.

	Van	Motor-bike	Car	Total
Travelling North	15			48
Travelling South	20		23	
Total		21		100

Fill in the table as you answer each question.

Use the table to answer the following questions.

a) How many **vans** were recorded in total? ....

b) How many vehicles were travelling **south**? ....

c) How many **motorbikes** were travelling **south**? ....

d) How many **cars** were travelling **north**? ....

For any two-way table, the total of all the rows should be the same as the total of all the columns. If they're not, double check that your numbers are right.

Scatter Graphs

Q1 The scatter graphs A, B and C below show how the number of ice creams sold is affected by the **temperature**, the **price** of the ice cream, and the **age** of the customers:

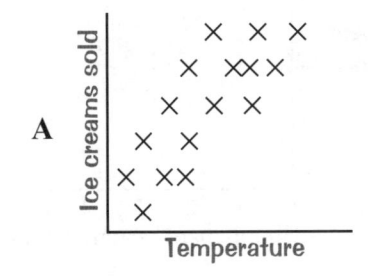

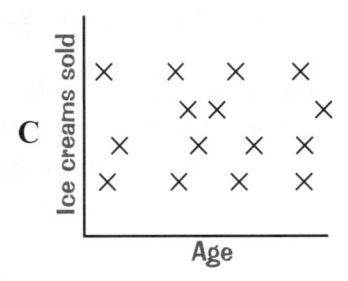

Fill in the spaces below with the letter A, B or C to say which graph shows which type of correlation.

Graph .... shows no correlation.

Graph .... shows positive correlation.

Graph .... shows negative correlation.

Q2 The table below shows the shoe sizes and heights for 12 pupils in a class.

Shoe size	5	6	4	6	7	7	8	3	5	9	10	10
Height (cm)	155	157	150	159	158	162	162	149	152	165	167	172

On the grid below, draw a scatter graph to show this information.

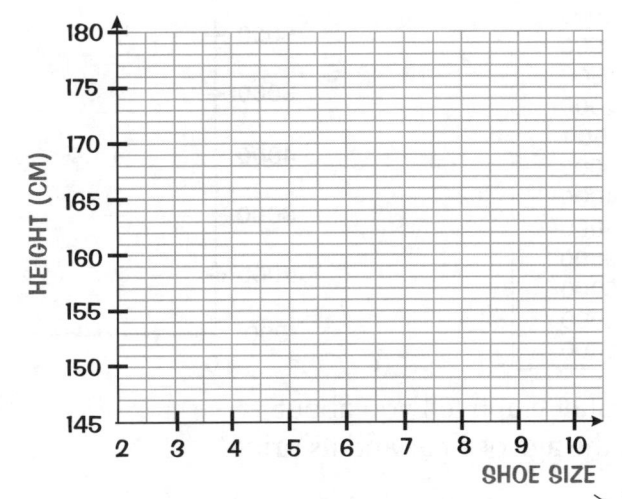

a) Draw a **line of best fit** on your scatter graph.

b) What does this scatter graph tell you about the link between **shoe size** and **height**?

A line of best fit is a straight line that goes through the middle of all the points.

....

....

SECTION FIVE — HANDLING DATA

Scatter Graphs

Q3 The scatter graph on the right shows how much time a group of people spent **doing sport** and **playing computer games** on one day.

Match the **points** labelled A, B and C on the scatter graph to each of the **people** below by writing A, B or C in the spaces.

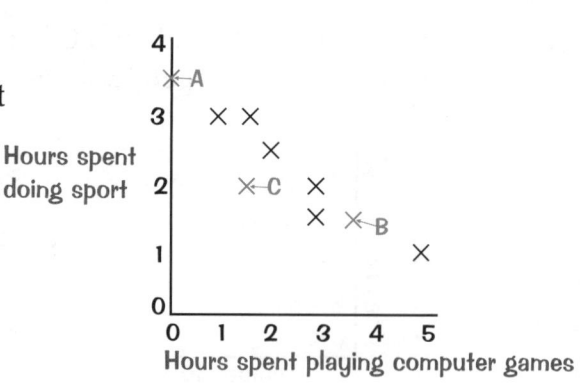

a) *The rugby practice was a long one so I didn't have much time to play on the computer.*

Point ....

b) Point .... *I don't have a computer!*

c) Point .... *I went to visit a friend. We played a bit of football then spent most of the evening playing his new computer game.*

Q4 Alice wrote down the **ages** and **prices** of 15 used cars on sale in her area, as shown in the table below. On the grid below, **draw a scatter graph** to show this information.

Age of car (years)	Price (£)
4	5000
2	8000
3	6500
1	8000
5	3500
8	4500
9	2000
1	7500
2	8000
6	4000
5	4000
1	9000
3	6000
4	4000
9	2000

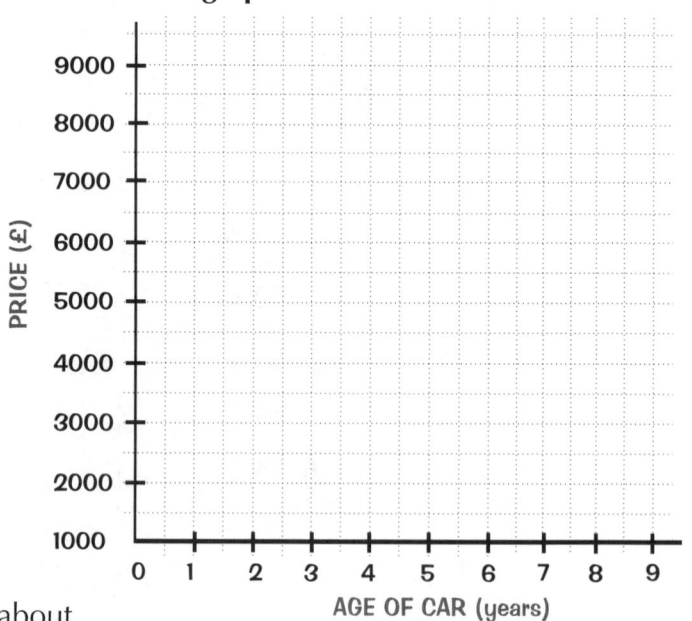

a) What does the scatter graph tell you about the link between the **age** of a car and its **price**?

....

b) Draw a line of best fit on the graph, and use it to find how much an **8-year-old** car is likely to cost Alice: £......................

The important word in scatter graph questions is CORRELATION —
so <u>use it</u> when you're asked to talk about the <u>relationship</u> between things.

SECTION FIVE — HANDLING DATA

Bar Charts

Q1 The **bar chart** on the right shows the favourite colours of students in a class.

Use the bar chart to answer the following questions:

a) How many students like **blue** best? ....

b) How many **more** people chose **red** than **yellow**? ....

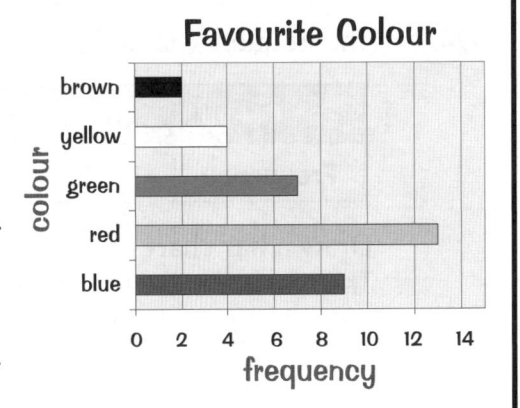

c) How many students were there **in total**? ....

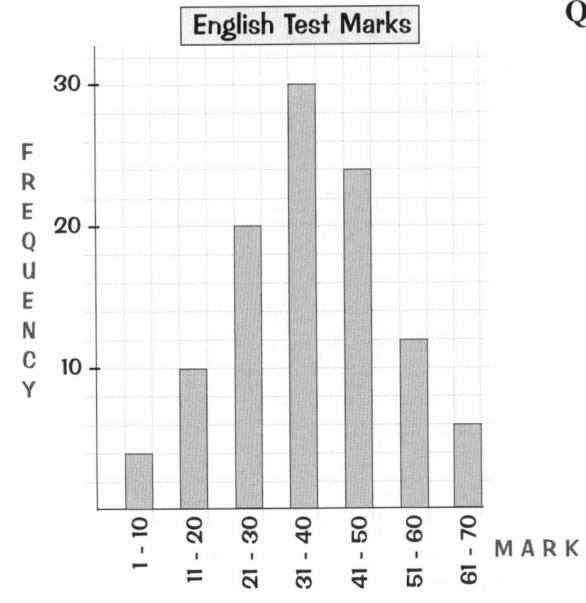

Q2 The **bar chart** on the left shows how a group of people scored on an English test.

a) How many people scored between **1 and 10**?

....

b) How many people scored **20 marks or less**?

....

c) The pass mark for this test was **31**. How many people **passed** the test?

....

d) How many people took the test **in total**?

....

Q3 The **dual bar chart** on the right shows how many people ordered pizza and pasta in a café over one week.

a) On which days was **pizza** more popular than pasta?

....

....

b) On which day did the café serve the **most meals**?

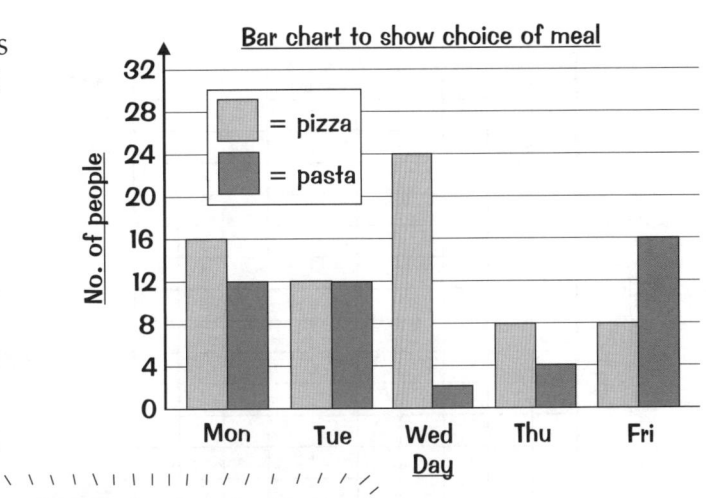

....

Add the two bars together for each day to find how many customers there were that day.

SECTION FIVE — HANDLING DATA

Bar Charts

Q4 The frequency table below shows the eye colour of 50 people who buy new glasses:

Eye Colour	Blue	Brown	Green	Hazel	Grey
Frequency	16	22	7	3	2

Draw a bar chart on the grid below to show the information in the table. The first bar has been drawn for you.

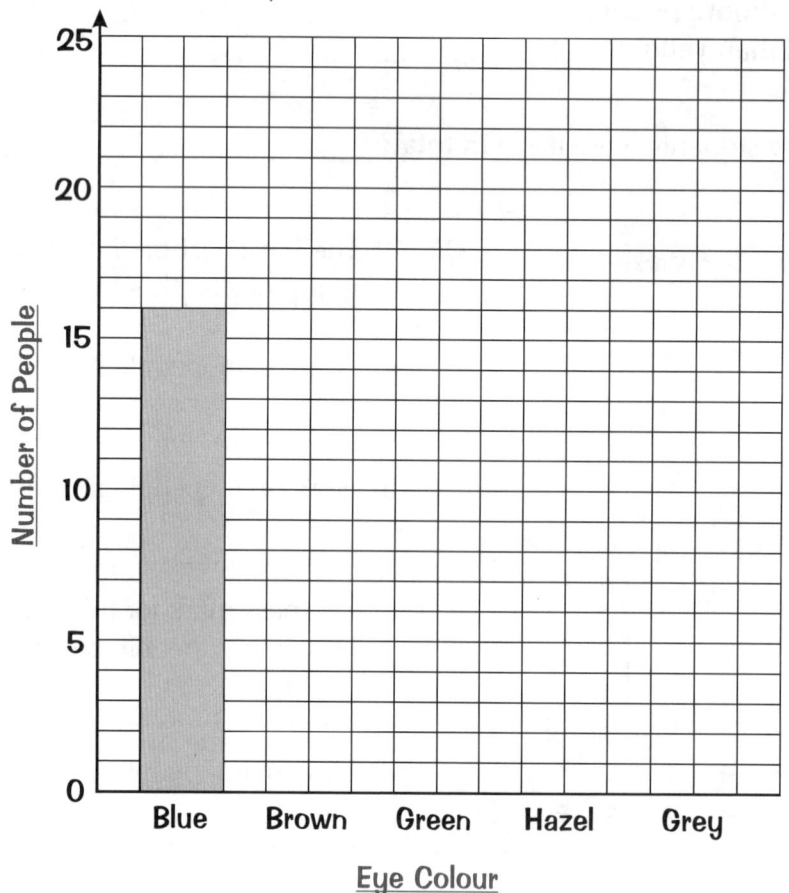

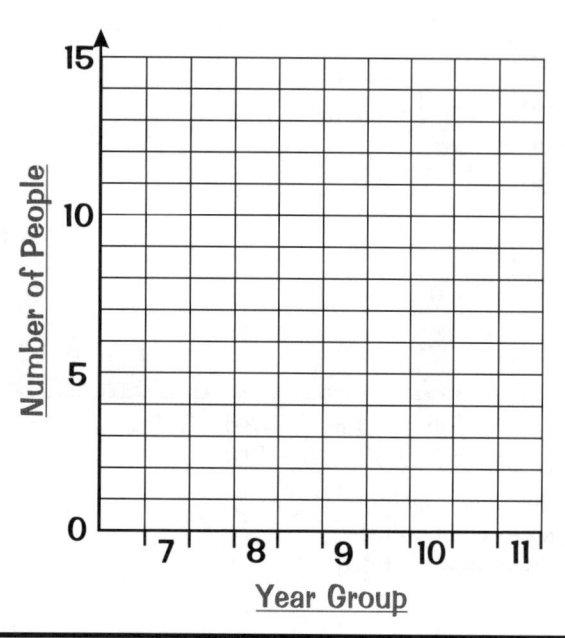

Q5 **Complete the bar chart** on the left using the information in the table below to show the year group of youth club members.

Year Group	Frequency
7	5
8	7
9	12
10	4
11	2

Pie Charts

Q1 The **table** and **pie chart** below show how long each type of TV programme is shown on one channel on one day.

Programme	Hours	Angle
News	5	75°
Sport	3	
Music	2	
Documentary	3	
Comedy	2	
Other	9	
Total	24	360°

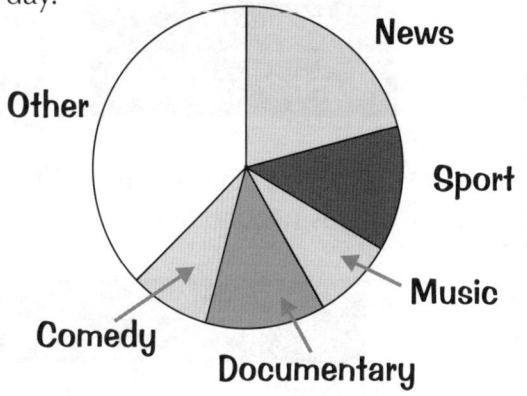

Use a protractor (angle measurer) to find the **size of the angle** for each part of the chart. Fill in the table with the angles you measure. The first angle has been done for you.

Q2 Sandra has drawn a **pie chart** (below) to show how much money her company spends on different things. The company spends **£54 000** each week in total.

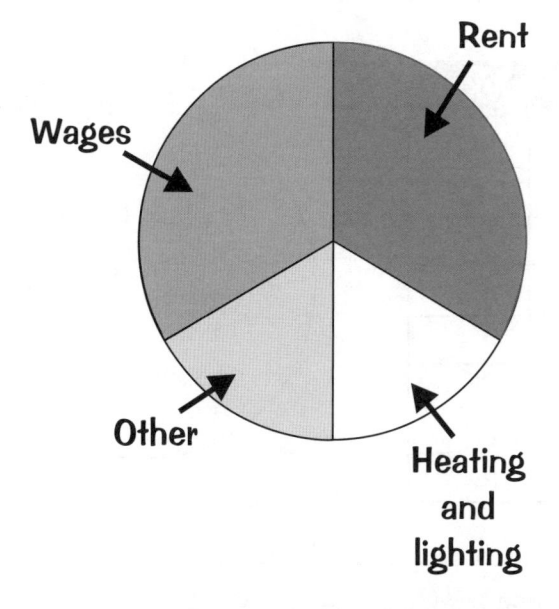

a) What **fraction** of the money goes on **wages**?

....

b) **How much** money goes on wages each week?

....

c) How much money is spent on **heating and lighting** each week?

....

....

The 'heating and lighting' bit of the pie is half the size of the 'wages' bit, so use this to answer part c).

SECTION FIVE — HANDLING DATA

Pie Charts

Q3 In a company there are **180 people** from different countries.

Country	UK	Malaysia	Spain	Others
Number of people	90	35	10	45

a) Fill in the blanks in the table below to find the **angles** needed to draw a pie chart of the data.

COUNTRY	WORKING	ANGLE
UK	90 ÷ 180 × 360	180°
MALAYSIA	35 ÷ 180 × 360	70°
SPAIN	.... ÷ 180 × 360	20°
OTHERS	45 ÷ 180 × 360	....

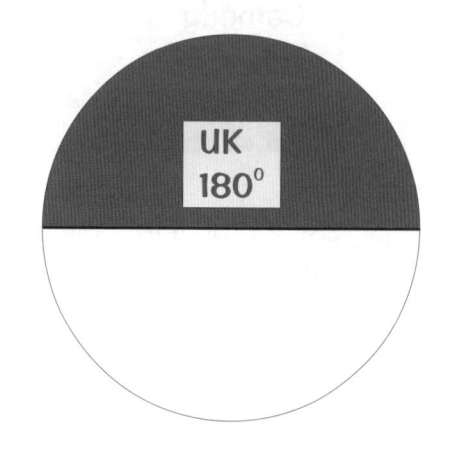

b) Complete the pie chart on the right by **drawing in the angles** from the table using a protractor (angle measurer). The UK part has been done for you.

UK 180°

Q4 Paul recorded how he spent his time one weekend. His results are shown in the table below.

ACTIVITY	HOURS	WORKING	ANGLE
Homework	6	6 ÷ 48 × 360 =	45°
Sport	2	2 ÷ 48 × 360 =	15°
TV	10	10 ÷ 48 × 360 =	
Computer games	2	2 ÷ 48 × 360 =	
Sleeping	18		
Listening to music	2		
Paid work	8		
Total	48		360°

a) Complete the table to work out the angles for each section of the pie chart.

b) Use the angles found in part **a)** to **draw and label** each section of the pie chart on the circle above using a protractor.

All the angles in the full circle should add up to 360°.
You shouldn't have any gaps when you draw in the parts of the pie chart.

SECTION FIVE — HANDLING DATA

SECTION SIX — GRAPHS

X and Y Coordinates

Q1 On the grid **plot** the points below and **label** them with the letters A-S.
Join the points with straight lines as you plot them.

A(0, 8) B(4, 6) C(4.5, 6.5) D(5, 6) E(9, 8) F(8, 5.5)

G(5, 5) H(8, 4) I(7.5, 2) J(6, 2) K(5, 4) L(4.5, 3.5)

M(4, 4) N(3, 2) O(1.5, 2) P(1, 4) Q(4, 5) R(1, 5.5) S(0, 8).

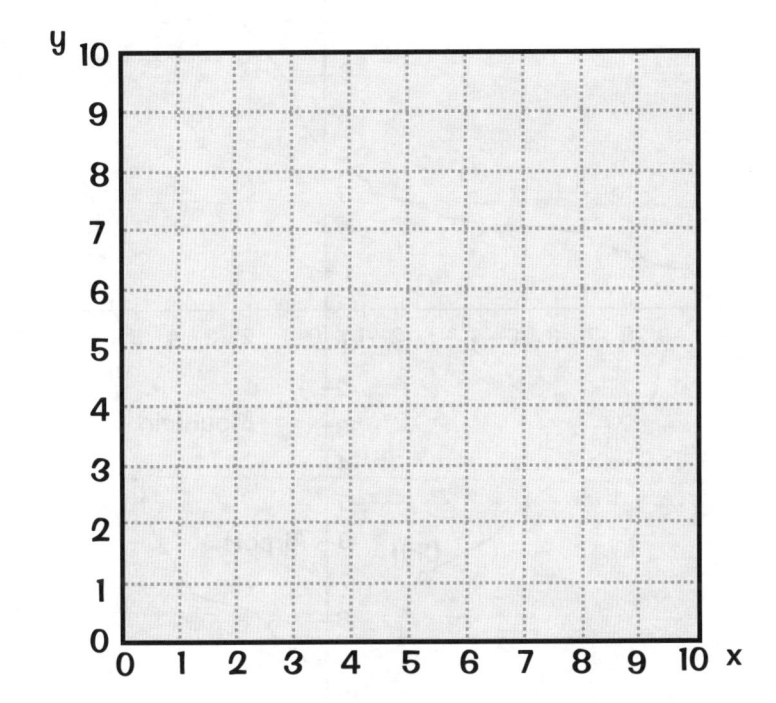

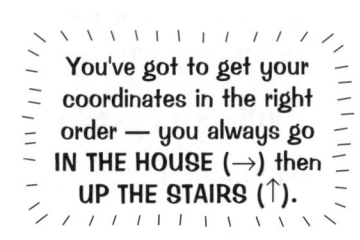

You've got to get your coordinates in the right order — you always go IN THE HOUSE (→) then UP THE STAIRS (↑).

You should see the outline of an **insect**. What is it? ....

Q2 Write down the **letter** that's next to each of the points on the grid below.
The sentence it spells is the answer to question one. One has been done for you.

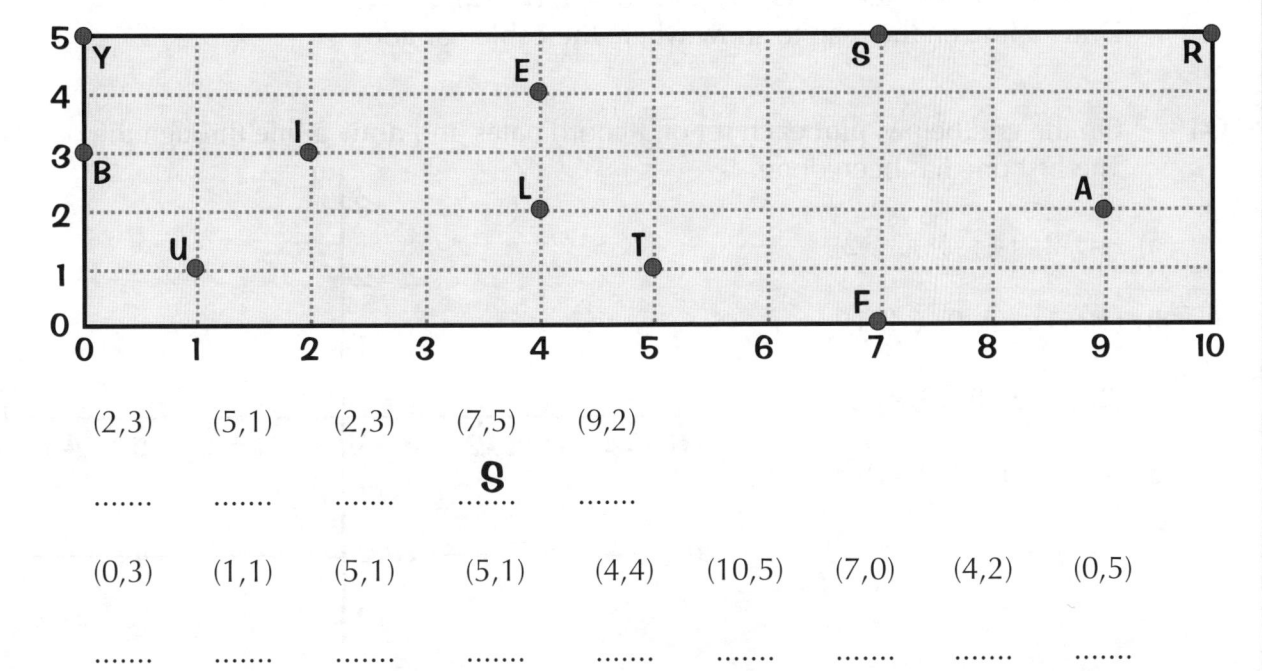

(2,3) (5,1) (2,3) (7,5) (9,2)
....   S   ......

(0,3) (1,1) (5,1) (5,1) (4,4) (10,5) (7,0) (4,2) (0,5)
....

SECTION SIX — GRAPHS

X and Y Coordinates

Remember — 1) x comes before y
2) x goes a-cross the page (get it).

Q3 The map on the right shows an island.

a) Use the map to write down the **coordinates** of these places:

Airport (...... , ...)

Mountain (...... , ...)

Beach (...... , ...)

City (...... , ...)

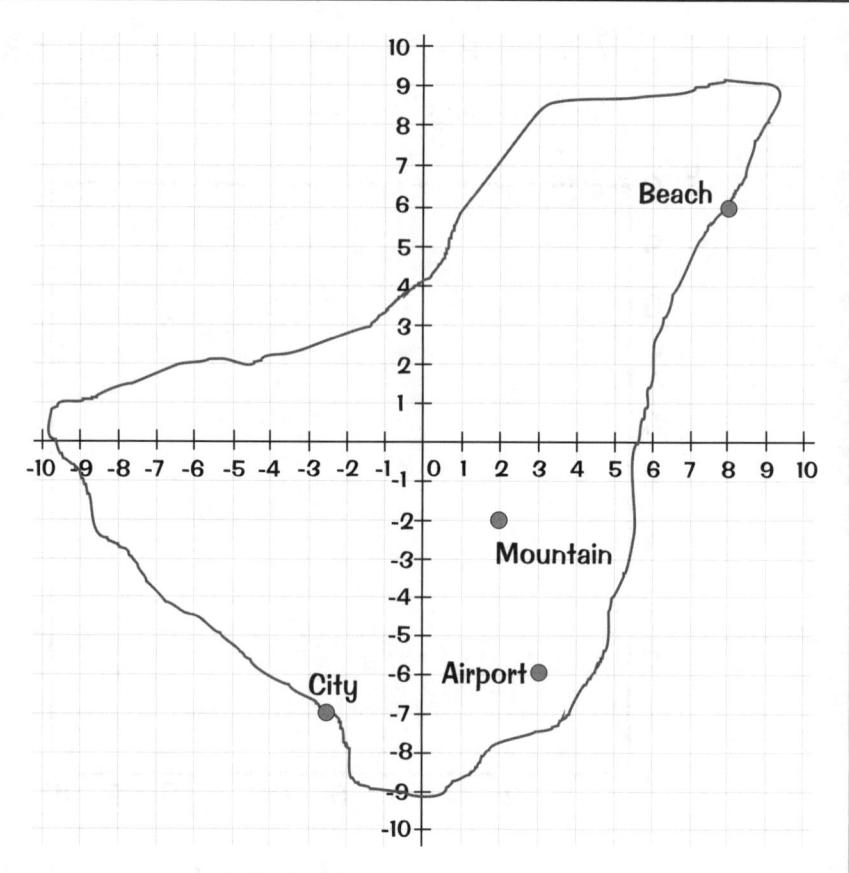

b) Mark these places on the map using their coordinates:
Shopping Centre **(-4 , -6)**, Village **(4 , -4)**, Park **(-6 , 2)**, Diving School **(9 , 9)**.

c) A cable car ride starts at **(3 , 1)** and ends at **(2 , -2)**.
Draw a **line** on the map to show where the cable car goes.

Q4 On the grid below, **plot** each set of 3 coordinates and **draw a line** through the points. The first one has been done.

a) (-4, -2), (-1, -2), (3, -2)

b) (-4, -1), (-4, 0), (-4, 1)

c) (2, 2), (0, 0), (-3, -3)

d) (-1, 2), (0, 1), (2, -1)

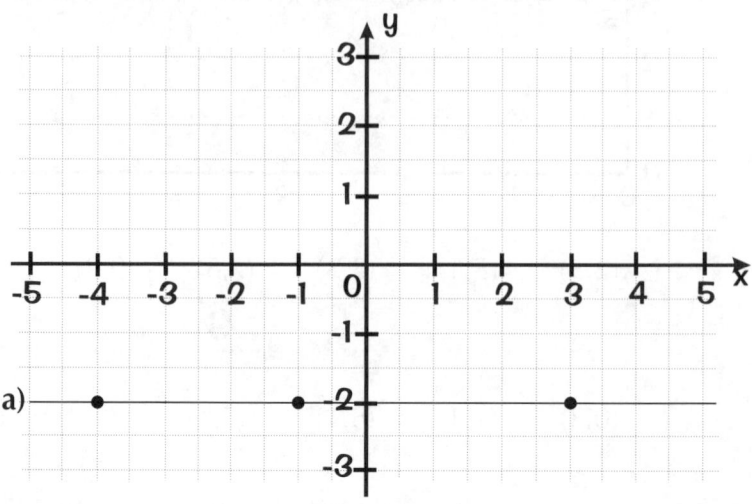

SECTION SIX — GRAPHS

Midpoint of a Line Segment

Q1 Write down the coordinates of the midpoints of the lines:

a) AB (......, ...)

b) CD (......, ...)

c) EF (......, ...)

d) GH (......, ...)

Q2 Write down the **midpoint of AB**, where A and B have the following coordinates:

Your answers should be coordinates too.

a) A(2, 3)   B(4, 5) ....

b) A(1, 8)   B(9, 2) ....

c) A(0, 11) B(12, 11) ....

d) A(3, 15) B(13, 3) ....

e) A(6, 6)   B(0, 0) ....

f) A(15, 9) B(3, 3) ....

Q3 Write down the coordinates of the **midpoints** of:

a) PQ, where P has coordinates **(1, 5)** and Q has coordinates **(5, 6)**.

b) AB, where A has coordinates **(3, 3)** and B has coordinates **(4, 0)**.

c) RS, where R has coordinates **(4, 5)** and S has coordinates **(0, 0)**.

d) PQ, where P has coordinates **(1, 3)** and Q has coordinates **(3, 1)**.

e) GH, where G has coordinates **(0, 0)** and H has coordinates **(-6, -7)**.

SECTION SIX — GRAPHS

Straight-Line Graphs

Keep learning these straight-line graphs until you know them off by heart — you've got to know about the **vertical and horizontal** lines and the **sloping** ones **through the origin**.

Q1 On the grid to the right:
- **a)** Label the *x* **axis**.
- **b)** Label the *y* **axis**.
- **c)** Draw and label the line *x* = 3.
- **d)** Draw and label the line *x* = -3.
- **e)** Draw and label the line *x* = 5.

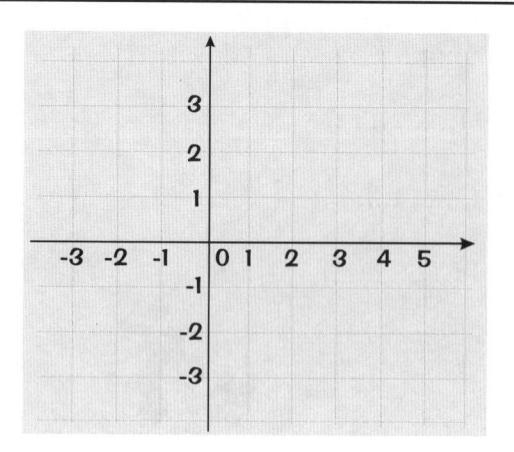

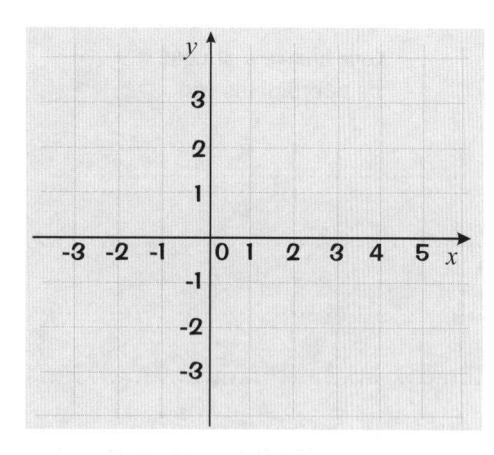

Q2 On the grid to the left:
- **a)** Label the line *x* = 0.
- **b)** Label the line *y* = 0.
- **c)** Draw and label the line *y* = 2.
- **d)** Draw and label the line *y* = -2.
- **e)** Draw and label the line *y* = -3.

Q3 On the grid below:
- **a)** Draw and label the line *y* = *x*.
- **b)** Draw and label the line *y* = -*x*.

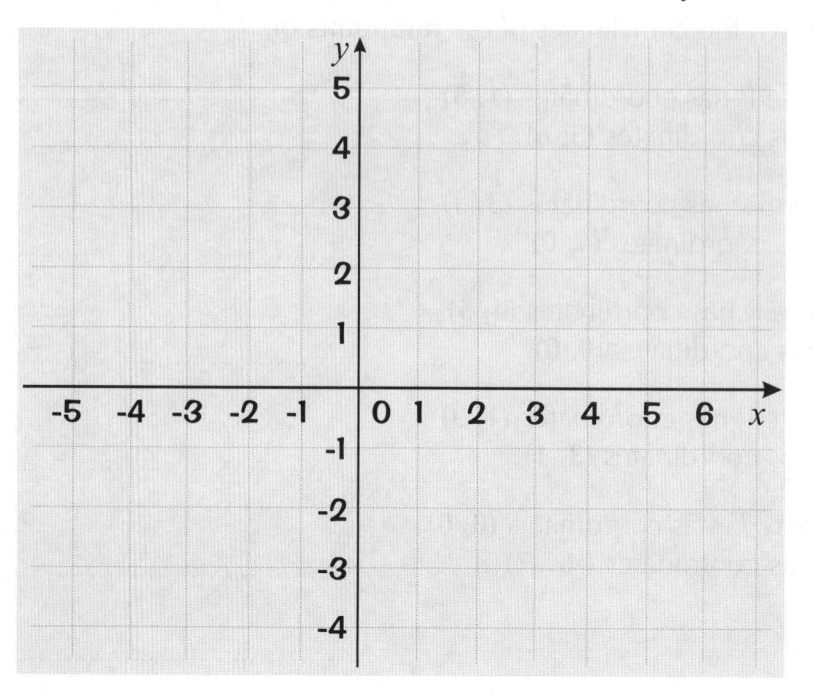

SECTION SIX — GRAPHS

Straight-Line Graphs

Q4 Write down the **letter** of the line on the grid below which matches each of these equations:

a) $y = x$? ....

b) $x = 5$? ....

c) $y = -x$? ....

d) $x = 0$? ....

e) $y = -7$? ....

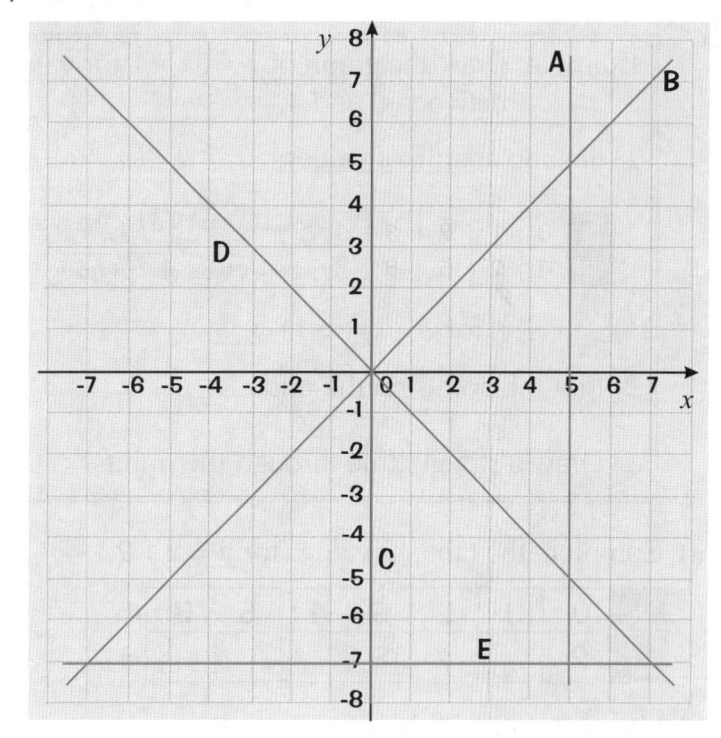

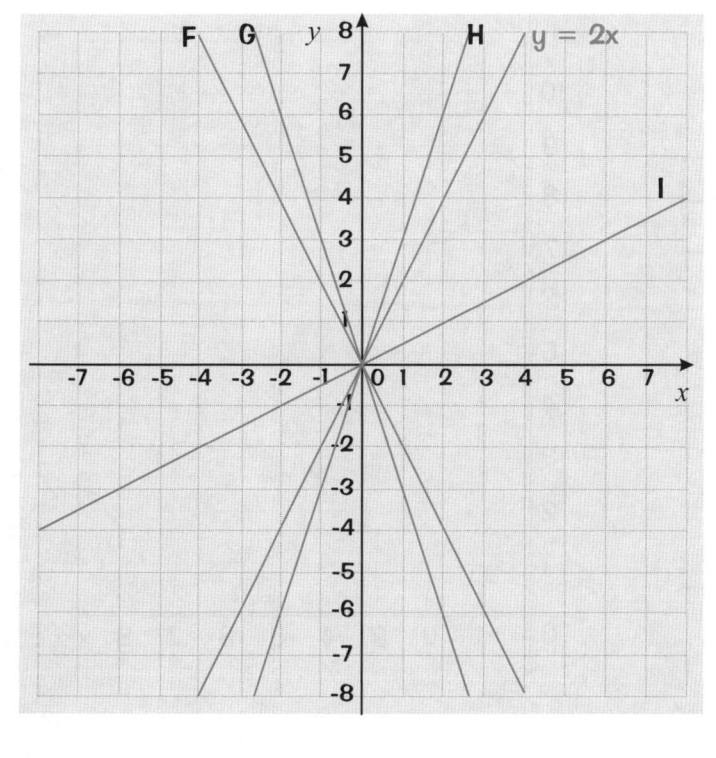

Q5 Write down the **letter** of the line on the grid to the left which matches each of these:

a) $y = -2x$? ....

b) $y = 3x$? ....

c) $y = -3x$? ....

Q6 Circle the equation below that matches **graph I**:

$y = 4x$ $y = ½x$

$y = -4x$ $y = -½x$

Q7 Circle all the equations below that make **straight-line graphs**:

$2y = \dfrac{1}{x}$ $y + x = 4$

$y = 2x + 5$ $y^2 = x - 3$ $y = 4x^2$

SECTION SIX — GRAPHS

Straight-Line Graphs

When you have to draw a graph from an equation, the very first thing to do is work out a table of values.

Example: Draw the graph of $y = 3x - 1$ for values of x between 0 and 4.

1) First do a table of values:

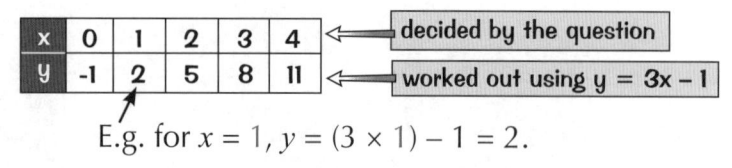

x	0	1	2	3	4
y	-1	2	5	8	11

← decided by the question
← worked out using $y = 3x - 1$

E.g. for $x = 1$, $y = (3 \times 1) - 1 = 2$.

2) Plot the points on the grid.

3) Draw a straight line through the points.

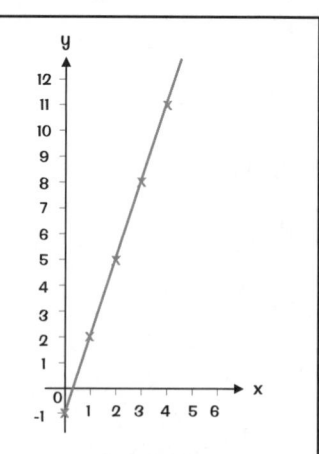

Q8 a) Complete the table of values for $y = x + 2$.

x	0	1	2	3	4	5	6
y	2			5			

b) Use your table of values to draw the **graph** of $y = x + 2$ on the grid opposite. Label the graph $y = x + 2$.

Q9 a) Fill in the table of values for $y = x - 1$.

x	1	2	3	4	5	6	7
y	0				4		

b) Use your table of values to draw the **graph** of $y = x - 1$ on the grid. Label the graph $y = x - 1$.

Q10 a) Complete the table for $y = 2x$.

x	0	1	2	3	4	5	6
y				6			12

b) Draw and label the **graph** of $y = 2x$ on the grid.

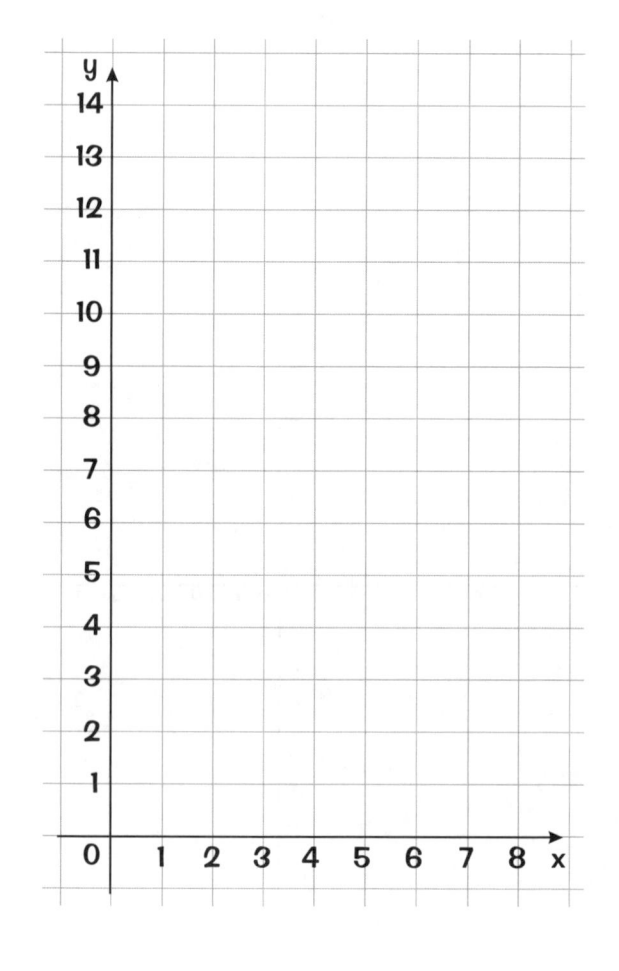

Q11 a) Fill in the table for $y = 8 - x$.

x	0	1	2	3	4	5	6
y	8			5			2

b) Draw and label the **graph** of $y = 8 - x$ on the grid.

SECTION SIX — GRAPHS

Straight-Line Graphs

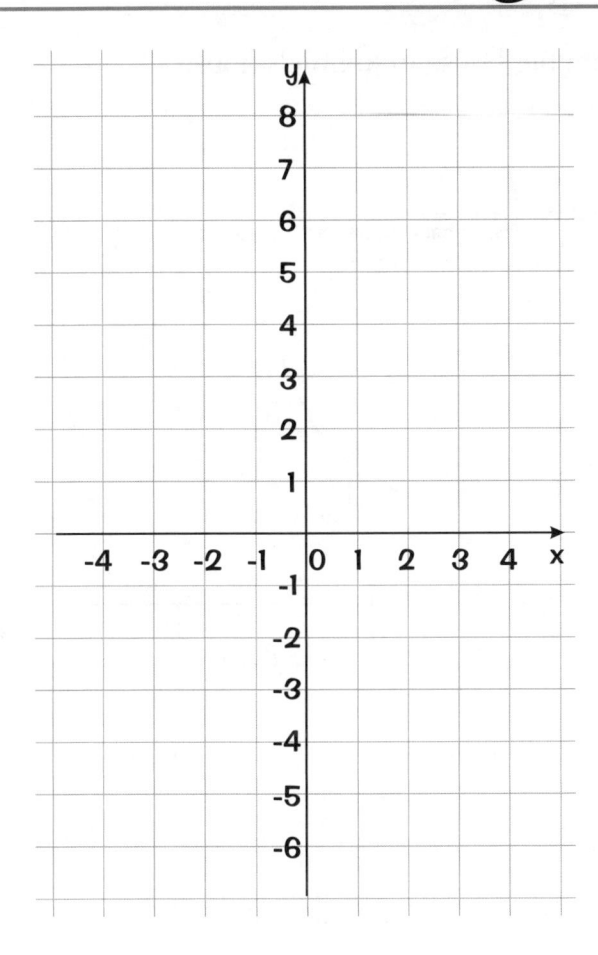

Q12 a) Complete the table of values for $y = x + 3$.

x	-3	-2	-1	0	1	2	3
y	0			3			

b) Draw and label the **graph** of $y = x + 3$ on the grid on the left.

Q13 a) Fill in the table of values for $y = x - 2$.

x	-3	-2	-1	0	1	2	3
y	-5			-2			

b) Draw and label the **graph** of $y = x - 2$ on the grid on the left.

Q14 a) Fill in the table for $y = x + 4$.

x	-3	-2	-1	0	1	2	3
y							

b) Draw and label the **graph** of $y = x + 4$ on the grid on the left.

Q15 a) Fill in the table of values for $y = 3x$.

x	-2	-1	0	1	2
y	-6				6

b) Draw the **graph** of $y = 3x$ on the grid on the right.

Q16 a) Complete the table of values for $y = 2x + 1$.

x	-3	-2	-1	0	1	2	3
y	-5			1			7

b) Draw the **graph** of $y = 2x + 1$ on the grid on the right.

Q17 a) Fill in the table of values for $y = 2x - 1$.

x	-2	-1	0	1	2	3	4
y	-5						7

b) Draw the **graph** of $y = 2x - 1$ on the grid on the right.

SECTION SIX — GRAPHS

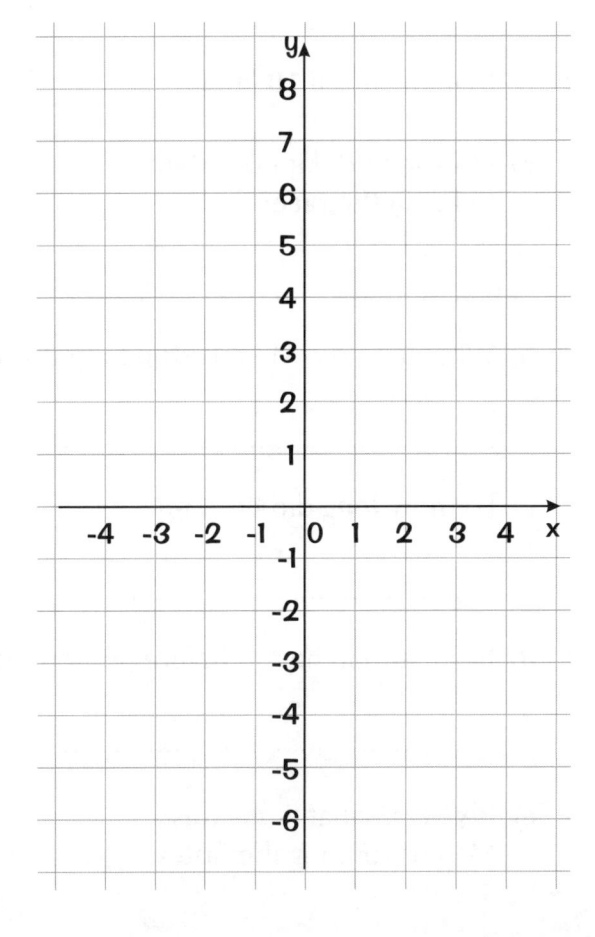

Travel Graphs

Q1 The graph below shows Nicola's journey from her house to **Robbie's house**, then to **Alan's house**, then **back home**.

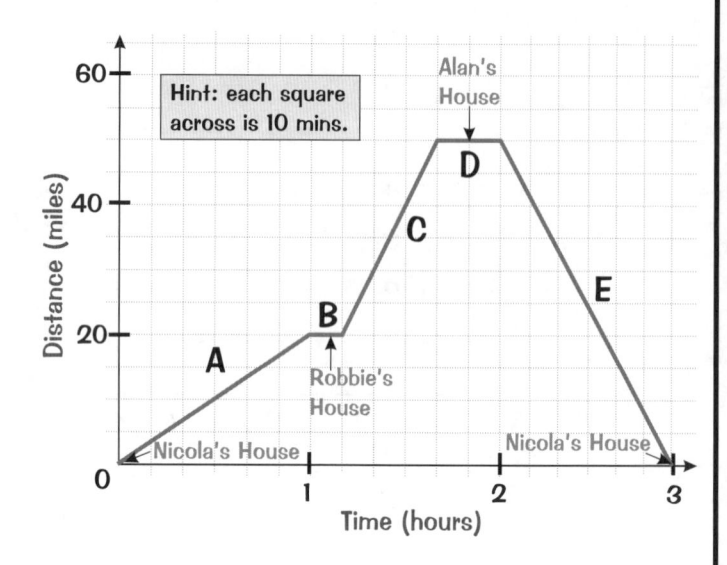

a) Nicola set off at **10.00 am**. What time did she get back home?

....

b) How far is **Robbie's house** from Nicola's?

....

c) How long did she **stop at Alan's** for?

....

d) How far is **Alan's house** from Nicola's? ....

e) How long did the **journey back** from Alan's take? ....

f) Give the letter of the **fastest** section of the journey. ....

Q2 Marcus runs a **10 km** race. A travel graph of his race is shown below.

a) How long did it take Marcus to **finish the race**?

....

b) What time did Marcus **stop** for a drink?

....

c) For **how long** did he stop?

....

d) How far had he run **before** he stopped?

....

e) Between what times was Marcus running the **fastest**? ....

SECTION SIX — GRAPHS

Travel Graphs

Q3 The travel graph below shows the start of Ari's journey to school. Complete the graph to show the following:

a) 8.10 - 8.15: she **stops** at the shop.

b) 8.15 - 8.20: she runs **back home** to get her homework.

c) 8.25 - 8.35: she runs from home to **school**.

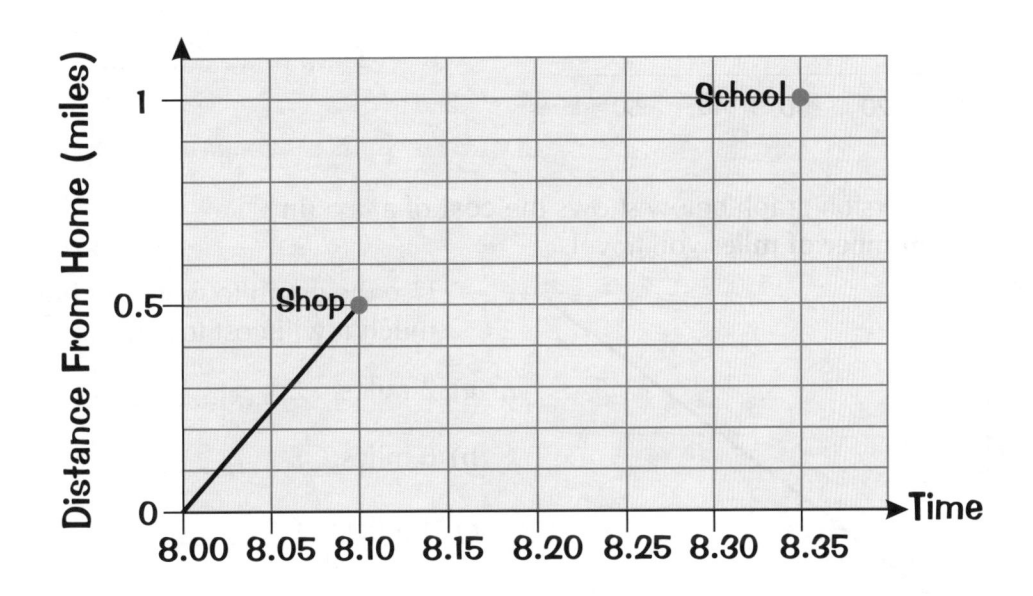

Q4 Draw a travel graph on the grid below to show the following journey:

Lyn jogs <u>5 km</u> at a steady speed for <u>15 minutes</u>...

...then <u>stops</u> for <u>5 minutes</u>...

...then <u>runs back</u> to the start in <u>10 minutes</u>.

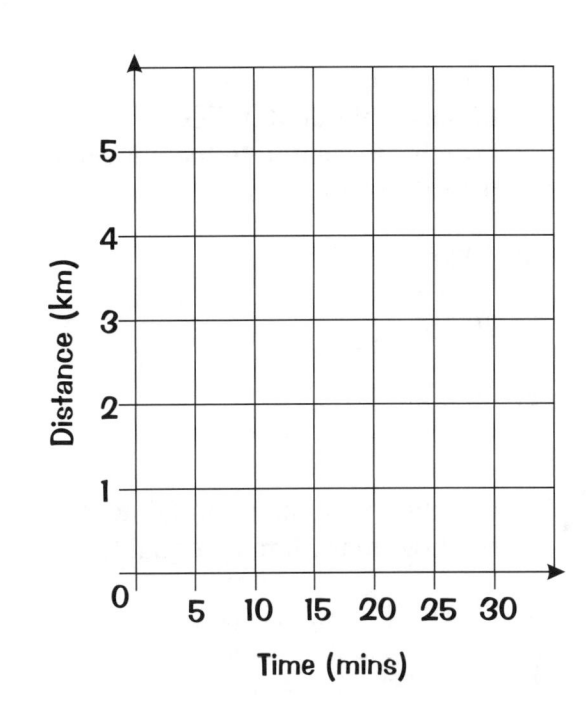

SECTION SIX — GRAPHS

Conversion Graphs

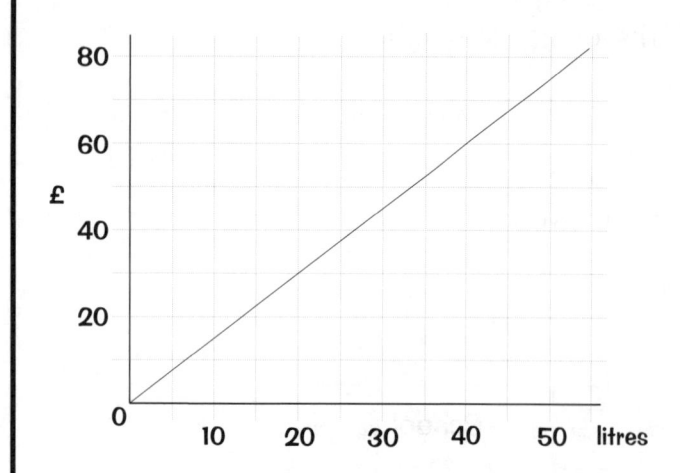

Q1 The conversion graph on the left shows how much it costs for an amount of petrol.

Use the graph to work out how much it will cost for **40 litres** of petrol.

£..................................

Q2 The conversion graph below shows the **cost** of a taxi (in £) for the **number of miles** you travel.

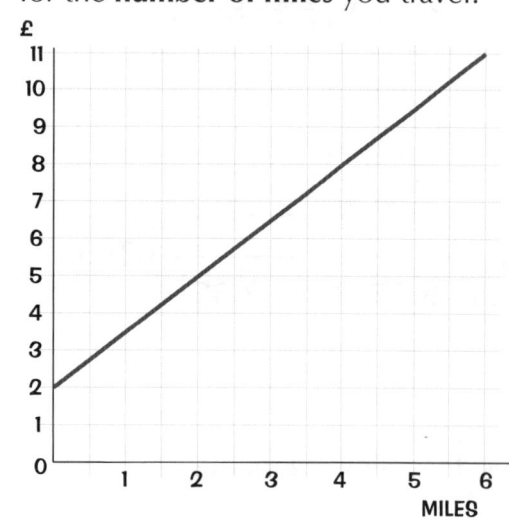

Use the graph to work out how much it will cost to travel:

a) 2 miles: £....................

b) 6 miles: £....................

c) 3 miles: £....................

d) Use the graph to work out how many miles you could travel in a taxi for **£8**.

.... miles

Q3 **80 km** is about **50 miles**.
Use this to **complete the conversion graph** below, then find how many miles are equal to:

a) 40 km ....

b) 20 km ....

c) 60 km ....

Plot the point on the grid where 50 miles meets 80 km, then join it with a straight line to (0, 0).

Q4 Use the graph drawn in **Q3** to work out how many **km** are equal to:

a) 25 miles ....

b) 10 miles ....

c) 5 miles ....

SECTION SIX — GRAPHS

Reading Off Graphs

To read off a graph, whether it's a straight line or a curve, follow this method:

- Draw a <u>straight line</u> to the graph from <u>one axis</u>.
- Then draw a straight line <u>down or across to the other axis</u>.

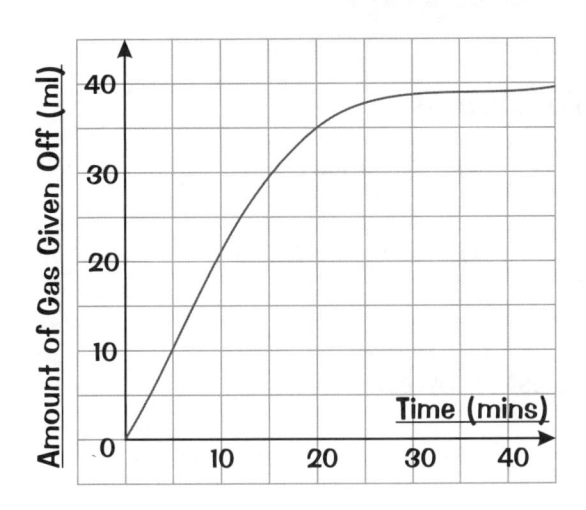

Q1 The graph on the left shows the results of a science experiment. Use the graph to answer the following:

a) How much gas was given off after **20 minutes**?

.... ml

b) How long did it take for **10 ml** of gas to be given off?

.... mins

Q2 The graph on the right shows how the number of poodles in a town has grown over time. Use the graph to answer the following:

a) How many years did it take for there to be **200 poodles**?

....

b) How many poodles were there after **6 years**?

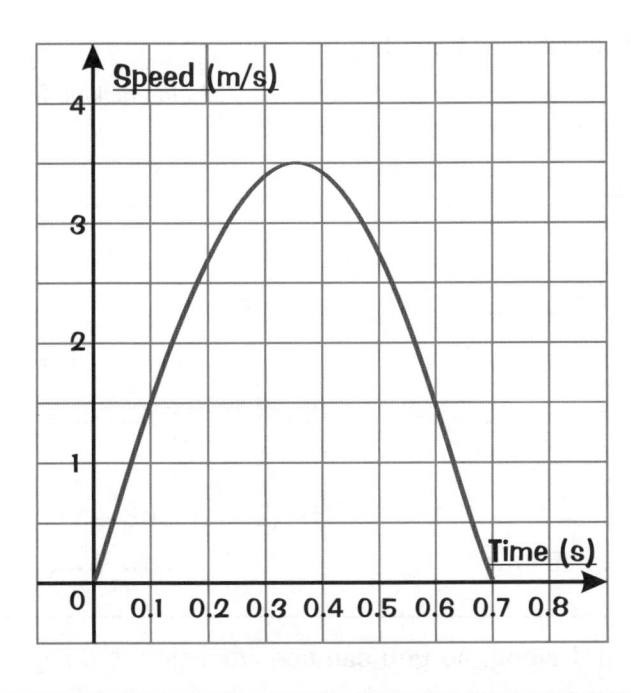

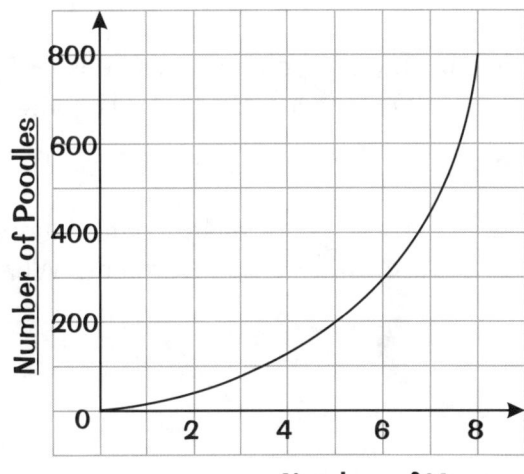

....

Q3 The graph on the left shows the speed of a toy car as it speeds up and slows down. Use the graph to answer the following:

a) At what times was it going at a speed of **1.5 m/s**?

.... s and .... s

b) What was its **highest** speed?

.... m/s

SECTION SIX — GRAPHS

Negative Numbers

Q1 Write these numbers in the right places on the **number line** below:

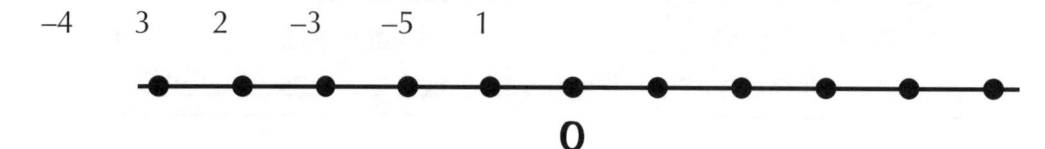

−4 3 2 −3 −5 1

0

Q2 **Circle** the **higher** number in each of the following pairs:

a) 4   −8   b) −6   −2   c) −8   −7

d) −3   −6   e) −1   1   f) −3.6   −3.7

Q3 Put these numbers in order of size, from **highest to lowest**:

−2   2   0.5   −1.5   −8   ....

Q4 a) The temperature outside is −3 °C, but will be −5 °C in a few hours. Does this mean that it is going to get colder or warmer?

....

b) In a different country, the temperature is −4 °C and will **drop** by **5 °C** overnight. What will the temperature be overnight?

.......................°C

Answer the following questions **without** using your calculator.

Remember to do any bits in brackets first.

Q5 Work out:

a) -6 × 1 = ...   b) -8 + 12 = ...   c) -8 ÷ 8 = ...

d) -70 − 3 = ...   e) -100 ÷ 10 = ... f) 5 × -2 = ...

g) -6 × -11 = ...   h) -18 ÷ -6 = ...   i) -1 + -6 = ...

j) 27 ÷ -3 = ...   k) (12 − 8) ÷ -4   l) (2 − 3) × (-8 + 1)
                                = ... = ...   = ... = ...

It can help to draw a number line to count along, so you can see what you're doing.

Powers and Letters

Q1 Complete these sums by **filling in the blanks**:

a) $2^4 = 2 \times 2 \times 2 \times 2 =$ ....

b) $10^3 = 10 \times 10 \times 10 =$ ....

c) $3^4 =$ .... = ...

d) $6^4 =$ .... = ...

e) $1^6 =$ .... = ...

f) $5^3 =$ .... = ...

Q2 **Fill in the blanks** to write the following as numbers (the first one has been done for you):

a) Three to the power five = $3 \times 3 \times 3 \times 3 \times 3 = 3^5$

b) Four to the power six = ... = ...

c) Seven squared = ... = ...

d) Twelve cubed = ... = ...

Q3 **Simplify** the following:

a) $2 \times 2 \times 2 \times 2 \times 2 \times 2 \times 2 \times 2 =$ ....

b) $12 \times 12 \times 12 \times 12 \times 12 =$ ....

c) $m \times m \times m =$ ....

d) $y \times y \times y \times y =$ ....

e) $n \times n \times 2 =$ ....

f) $b \times a \times b \times 4 =$ ....

g) $c \times c \times d \times c \times a \times d =$ ....

h) $p \times p \times q \times q =$ ....

i) $(k - l) \times (k - l) =$ ....

j) $(s + t) \times (s + t) \times (s + t) =$ ....

Q4 Use your **calculator** to work out:

a) 4^3 ....
b) 10^4 ....
c) 12^5 ....
d) 13^3 ....

Q5 Work these out **without** using your calculator:

a) $-2^2 = -(2 \times 2) =$ ....

b) $(-2)^2 = -2 \times -2 =$ ....

c) $-3^2 =$ .... = ...

d) $(-3)^2 =$ .... = ...

Powers are a way of writing numbers in a shorter way. They're useful for big numbers. Imagine writing out 2^{138} — $2 \times 2 \times ... \times 2 \times ... \times 2 \times$ yawn $\times$ zzz...

SECTION SEVEN — ALGEBRA

Square Roots

- Square root just means "What Number Times by Itself Gives..."
- The square roots of 64 are 8 and –8 because 8 × 8 = 64 and –8 × –8 = 64.
- Square roots always have a + and – answer.

Q1 Use the $\sqrt{}$ button on your calculator to find the following **positive** square roots to the **nearest whole number**.

a) $\sqrt{60}$ = ...   b) $\sqrt{19}$ = ...   c) $\sqrt{34}$ = ...

d) $\sqrt{200}$ = ...   e) $\sqrt{520}$ = ...   f) $\sqrt{75}$ = ...

g) $\sqrt{750}$ = ...   h) $\sqrt{0.9}$ = ...   i) $\sqrt{170}$ = ...

j) $\sqrt{7220}$ = ...   k) $\sqrt{1\,000\,050}$ = ...   l) $\sqrt{27}$ = ...

Answer all the questions below **without** using your calculator.

Q2 Write down **both square roots** for each of the following:

a) 4 ....   b) 16 ....   c) 9 ....

d) 49 ....   e) 25 ....   f) 100 ....

g) 144 ....   h) 64 ....   i) 81 ....

Q3 **16** is one square root of **256**.

Write down the **other** square root of **256**: ....

If $x^2 = 121$, then $x = +\sqrt{121}$ and $-\sqrt{121}$.

Q4 If $x^2 = 121$, what are the **two** possible values of x? ....

Q5 The square on the right has an area of **36 cm²**. What is the length of a **side** of the square?

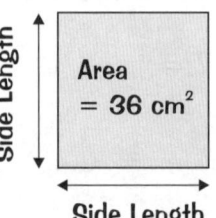

Area = 36 cm²

.... cm

The area of a square is the length of a side times by itself. So the side length is the square root of the area.

Section Seven — Algebra

Cube Roots

- Cube root means:
 "What Number Times by Itself Three Times Gives ..."
- The cube root of 27 is 3 because 3 × 3 × 3 = 27.
- Cube roots only have 1 answer.

Q1 Use the $\sqrt[3]{}$ button on your **calculator** to find the following:

a) $\sqrt[3]{4096}$ = ...

b) $\sqrt[3]{1728}$ = ...

c) $\sqrt[3]{1331}$ = ...

d) $\sqrt[3]{1\,000\,000}$ = ...

e) $\sqrt[3]{1}$ = ...

f) $\sqrt[3]{0.125}$ = ...

Answer all the questions below **without** using your calculator.

Q2 Find the value of the following:

a) $\sqrt[3]{64}$ = ...

b) $\sqrt[3]{27}$ = ...

c) $\sqrt[3]{1000}$ = ...

d) $\sqrt[3]{8}$ = ...

Q3 If $x^3 = 125$, what is x?

x × x × x = 125, so work out what number x must be.

....

Q4 The cube on the right has a volume of **8 cm³**. What is the length of a **side** of the cube?

.... cm

Volume = 8 cm³

The volume of a cube is the length of a side times by itself 3 times. So the side length is the cube root of the volume.

SECTION SEVEN — ALGEBRA

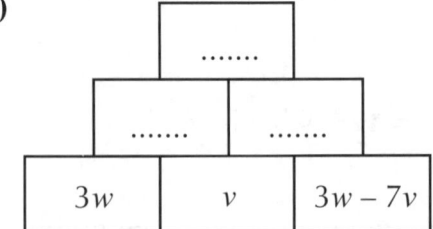

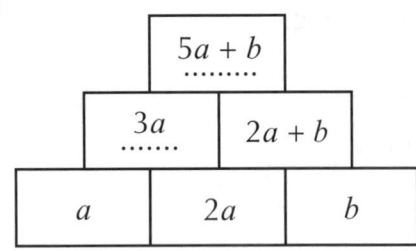

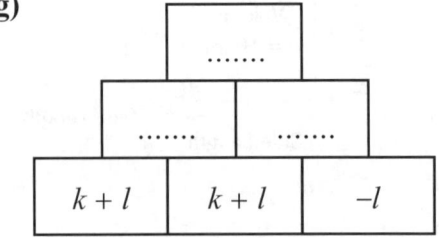

Algebra — Simplifying

Algebra can be pretty scary at first. But don't panic — the secret is just to practise lots and lots of questions.

Q1 Fill in the blank spaces in the pyramids so that the term in each block is found by **adding** the terms in the **two blocks below it**. The first one has been done for you.

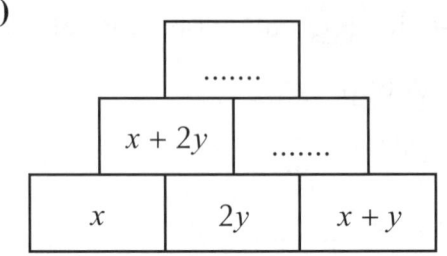

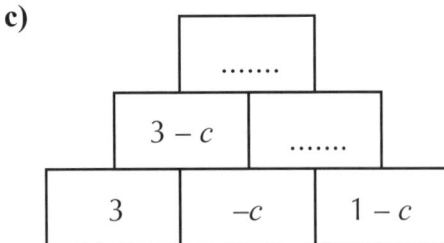

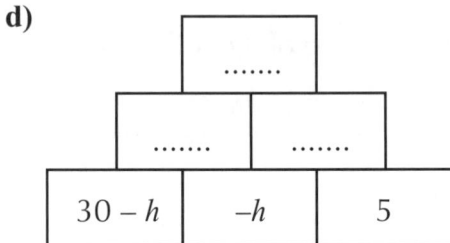

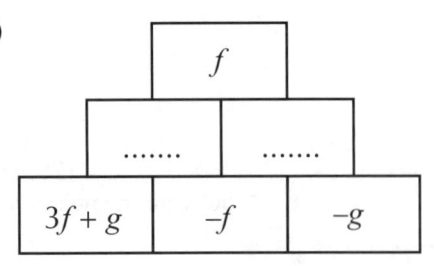

a)
```
        5a + b
    3a      2a + b
  a     2a      b
```

b)
```
        ......
    x + 2y    ......
  x     2y      x + y
```

c)
```
        ......
    3 – c     ......
  3     –c      1 – c
```

d)
```
        ......
    ......    ......
  30 – h    –h      5
```

e)
```
         f
    ......    ......
  3f + g    –f      –g
```

f)
```
        ......
    ......    ......
  3w     v      3w – 7v
```

g)
```
        ......
    ......    ......
  k + l    k + l    –l
```

h)
```
        ......
    ......    ......
  n + 2    10      m
```

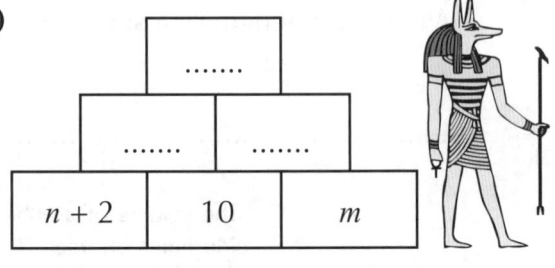

Algebra — Simplifying

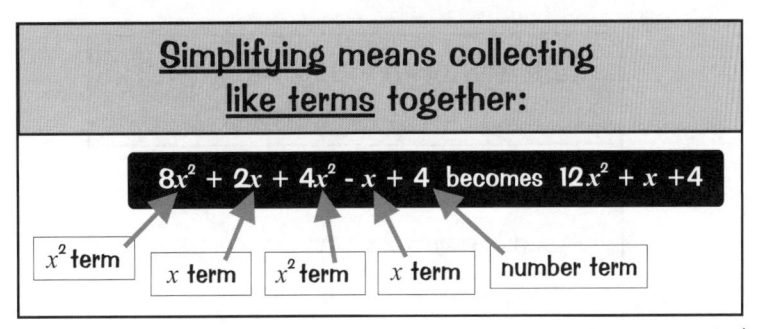

Simplifying means collecting like terms together:

$8x^2 + 2x + 4x^2 - x + 4$ becomes $12x^2 + x + 4$

- x^2 term
- x term
- x^2 term
- x term
- number term

Put 'bubbles' around each term, including the + or − sign, to help collect like terms.

Q2 Simplify the following expressions by **collecting like terms**. The first one has been done for you.

a) $6x + 3x - 5 = $ ....$9x - 5$........

b) $2x + 3x - 5x = $ ....

c) $9f + 16f + 15 - 30 = $ ....

d) $14x + 12x - 1 + 2x = $ ....

e) $3x + 4y + 12x - 5y = $ ....

f) $11a + 6b + 24a + 18b = $ ....

g) $9f + 16g - 15f - 30g = $ ....

h) $17a + 8a - 3 + 3a = $ ....

i) $4p + 3q - p + 2pq = $ ....

j) $5pq + pq + p = $ ....

k) $2xy + x + y - 2y = $ ....

l) $a^2 + ab - 2a^2 - 2ab = $ ....

Q3 Simplify the following expressions. The first one has been done for you.

An x² term is different to an x term — don't collect them together.

a) $3x^2 + 5x - 2 + x^2 - 3x = $ ....$4x^2 + 2x - 2$........

b) $5x^2 + 3 + 3x - 4 = $ ....

c) $13 + 2x^2 - 4x + x^2 + 5 = $ ....

d) $7y - 4 + 6y^2 + 2y - 1 = $ ....

e) $2a + 4a^2 - 6a - 3a^2 + 4 = $ ....

f) $15 - 3x - 2x^2 - 8 - 2x - x^2 = $ ....

g) $x^2 + 2x + x^2 + 3x + x^2 + 4x = $ ....

h) $2y^2 + 10y - 7 + 3y^2 - 12y + 1 = $ ....

i) $4p^2 + 1 - 3p - p^2 + 2 = $ ....

j) $5q + q^2 + 3q - 3q^2 + q = $ ....

k) $2x^2 + x + x - 2x^2 - 2x = $ ....

l) $a^2 + a - 2a^2 - 2b + a^2 - a = $ ....

SECTION SEVEN — ALGEBRA

Algebra — Brackets

> **Expanding means multiplying out brackets:**
>
> E.g. $4(x + y) = 4 \times (x + y) = 4x + 4y$
>
> $x(2 + x) = 2x + x^2$
>
> $-(a + b) = -a - b$

Careful with negative signs outside the brackets — they reverse the signs when you multiply.

Q1 Expand the brackets in the expressions below. The first one has been done for you.

a) $2(x + 3) = $ ......$2x + 6$......

b) $4(x - 2) = $ ....

c) $9(f + g) = $ ....

d) $x(x - 1) = $ ....

e) $3x(4 + x) = $ ....

f) $2a(6b + 4a) = $ ....

g) $9f(g - 3h) = $ ....

h) $-4(a + 12b^2) = $ ....

i) $-3p(3q - p) = $ ....

j) $-5p(q + r) = $ ....

k) $2(x^2 + x + y) = $ ....

l) $-a(b - 2b^2 - 2) = $ ....

Q2 Expand the brackets and then **simplify** the expressions. The first one has been done for you.

a) $2(x + y) + 3y = $ ......$2x + 2y + 3y = 2x + 5y$......

b) $4(x - 3) - 2 = $ ....

c) $8(x^2 + 2) - x^2 = $ ....

d) $-2(x + 5) + 2x = $ ....

e) $-(y - 2) + (y - 2) = $ ....

f) $x(y + 2) + xy = $ ....

g) $x(x + y + z) - x^2 + xy = $

....

h) $8(a + b) + 2(a + 2b) = $

....

Q3 Fill in the blanks to **factorise** the expressions below. Each has a **4** outside the bracket. The first one has been done for you.

a) $4x + 8 = 4($...$x + 2$...$)$

b) $12 - 8x = 4($..........$)$

c) $4 - 16x = 4($..........$)$

d) $4x^2 + 64 = 4($..........$)$

For each expression, decide what multiplies by 4 to get each term, then put it inside the bracket.

SECTION SEVEN — ALGEBRA

Number Patterns and Sequences

Q1 Draw the next **two** pictures in each pattern.
Write under each picture how many matchsticks have been used to make it.

a) , , , ,

....

b) , , , ,

....

                    ,

                ....

c) , , , ,

....

> Look for patterns in the numbers as well as in the pictures.

d) , , , ,

....

e) , , , ,

....

SECTION SEVEN — ALGEBRA

Number Patterns and Sequences

Q2 In each of the questions below, write down the next **three** numbers in the sequence and write the **rule** that you used.

> Once you've worked out the next numbers, go back and write down exactly what you did — that will be the rule you used.

a) 1, 3, 5, 7, ..., ..., ...

Rule ....

b) 2, 4, 8, 16, ..., ..., ...

Rule ....

c) 3, 30, 300, 3000, ..., ..., ...

Rule ....

d) 3, 7, 11, 15, ..., ..., ...

Rule ....

e) 4, 5, 7, 10, ..., ..., ...

Rule ....

f) 64, 32, 16, 8, ..., ..., ...

Rule ....

g) 45, 41, 37, 33, ..., ..., ...

Rule ....

h) 3, 6, 9, 15, 24, ..., ..., ...

Rule ....

Q3 The first five terms of a sequence are 3, 7, 11, 15, 19...
Is **34** a term in the sequence? Explain your answer.

....

....

To get the next number in the sequence, you usually have to add something, take something away, or multiply or divide by something.
There are also sequences where you add the last two terms together.

SECTION SEVEN — ALGEBRA

Formulas

A formula is like a set of step-by-step instructions written without using words. Formulas use letters in place of numbers, so you can substitute numbers in and see what you get back out.

Q1 If $x = 3$, find the value of the following expressions.

a) $x + 2$ ....   b) $2x$ ....   c) $x - 7$ ....

d) $x \div 3$ ....   e) $2x + 1$ ....   f) $3x - 4$ ....

Q2 If $y = 6$, find the value of the following expressions.

a) $2y + 2$ ....   b) $3y - 6$ ....   c) $4 + 2y$ ....

d) $20 - 3y$ ....   e) $2y \div 3$ ....   f) $4(1 + y)$ ....

Q3 Using the formula $z = x \div 5$, find the value of z when:

a) $x = 20$ ....   b) $x = 15$ ....

c) $x = 35$ ....

Q4 If $V = 2l + 6$ find V when:

a) $l = 7$ ....

b) $l = 12$ ....

Q5 If $V = 3 + 4t$, find the value of V when $t = 2$. ....

Q6 The cost in pounds (C) of hiring a bike depends on the number (n) of hours you use it for, where $C = 20 + 4n$. Find C when,

a) $n = 2$ ....   b) $n = 6$ ....

c) $n = 3.5$ ....

Q7 The time in minutes (t) taken to cook a chicken is given by the formula $t = 20w + 20$, where w is the chicken's weight in kg. Find the time needed to cook a chicken weighing:

a) 2 kg $t = $ .... = ... mins

b) 3.5 kg $t = $ .... = ... mins

SECTION SEVEN — ALGEBRA

Making Formulas from Words

Algebra is just normal maths, but with the odd letter or two thrown in there.

Q1 Steven is **16** years old. How old will he be in:

a) 5 years? .... b) 10 years? .... c) x years? ....

Q2 Tickets for a football match cost **£25** each. What is the cost for:

a) 2 tickets? ....

b) 6 tickets? ....

c) y tickets? ....

Q3 **Write a formula** to work out the value of y if it is:

a) Three more than x: $y =$ .... b) Seven less than x: $y =$ ....

c) Four multiplied by x: $y =$ .... d) x multiplied by x: $y =$ ....

e) Ten divided by x: $y =$ .... f) x divided by five: $y =$ ....

Q4 **Write a formula** to find the cost in pence (C) of printing n pages, if the cost per page is:

a) 4 pence: $C =$ ....

b) 5 pence: $C =$ ....

c) 12 pence: $C =$ ....

Q5 Ann is a years old. Her brother Ben is **2 years older** than Ann. Their sister Cat is **5 years younger** than Ann. **Write formulas** for:

a) Ben's age (b): $b =$ ....

b) Cat's age (c): $c =$ ....

Q6 The square on the right has side lengths d **cm**. **Write a formula** to work out p, the perimeter of the square.

$p =$ ....

Q7 The cost (C) of hiring a mountain bike is **£10**, plus **£5** for each hour you use the bike (h). Write down a formula to work out the cost, in pounds, of hiring a bike for h hours.

$C =$ ....

SECTION SEVEN — ALGEBRA

Solving Equations

To solve an equation, get the letter on its own ($x = ...$). You do this by adding, subtracting, multiplying, dividing... and you always have to do the same to both sides.

Q1 Solve these equations:

a) $a + 6 = 20$

a = ...

b) $b + 12 = 30$

b = ...

c) $3 + c = 7$

c = ...

d) $48 + d = 77$

d = ...

e) $397 + e = 842$

e = ...

f) $f + 9.8 = 14.1$

f = ...

Q2 Solve these equations:

a) $g - 7 = 4$

g = ...

b) $h - 14 = 11$

h = ...

c) $i - 38 = 46$

i = ...

d) $j - 647 = 353$

j = ...

e) $k - 6.4 = 2.9$

k = ...

f) $l - 7 = -4$

l = ...

Q3 Solve these equations:

a) $4m = 28$

m = ...

b) $7n = 84$

n = ...

c) $15p = 645$

p = ...

d) $279q = 1395$

q = ...

e) $6.4r = 9.6$

r = ...

f) $-5s = 35$

s = ...

Q4 Solve these equations:

a) $\frac{t}{3} = 5$

t = ...

b) $u \div 6 = 9$

u = ...

c) $\frac{v}{11} = 8$

v = ...

d) $\frac{w}{197} = 7$

w = ...

e) $x \div 1.8 = 7.2$

x = ...

f) $\frac{y}{-3} = 7$

y = ...

Q5 Melissa paid **£23.40** to download **three** albums of the same price.

a) How much did **each album** cost? .... = £..........

b) Each album contained **12 songs**. What was the price of each song? .... = £..........

Divide the total amount by 3 to find the price of each album, then divide that by 12 to find the price of each song.

SECTION SEVEN — ALGEBRA

Solving Equations

There's an extra step in these questions, so do the working out step-by-step.

Q6 **Solve** these equations:

a) $3x + 2 = 14$ .... $x =$ ....

b) $5x - 4 = 31$ .... $x =$ ....

c) $8 + 6x = 50$ .... $x =$ ....

d) $20 - 3x = -61$ .... $x =$ ....

Q7 **Solve** these equations:

a) $\frac{x}{3} + 4 = 10$ .... $x =$ ....

b) $\frac{x}{5} - 9 = 6$ .... $x =$ ....

c) $4 + \frac{x}{9} = 6$ .... $x =$ ....

d) $\frac{x}{17} - 11 = 31$ .... $x =$ ....

Multiply out the brackets first.

Q8 **Solve** these equations:

a) $3(2x + 1) = 27$ .... $x =$ ....

b) $4(2x + 1) = 36$ .... $x =$ ....

c) $6(x - 4) = 42$ .... $x =$ ....

d) $-2(-x + 6) = -10$ .... $x =$ ....

Q9 The cost of dry cleaning is **£2** per item of clothing, plus an overall charge of **£5**. Ken's dry cleaning cost **£13**. How many items of clothing did he have cleaned?

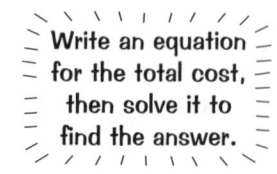

Write an equation for the total cost, then solve it to find the answer.

....

Q10 Florence booked **5** tickets for a concert. The total amount Florence paid was **£105**, but this included a **£5** postage cost. Work out the **cost** for each ticket **without** the postage cost.

....

SECTION SEVEN — ALGEBRA